Loving, Happy, Healthy, Wealthy, and Wise

A Spiritual Blueprint to Unlocking Life's Miracles

Steven Ernest Morrow

Loving, Happy, Healthy, Wealthy, and Wise: A Spiritual Bluprint to Unlocking Life's Miracles

Published by Peaceful Tree Publishing
Denver, CO

ISBN: 979-8-218-88207-5
RELIGION / Spirituality
SELF-HELP / Spiritual

Scripture quotations taken from the King James Version unless otherwise identified.

Contents

Whatever you think, feel, say, or do becomes you, because whatever happens to you happens through you.

Did You Know

You have been talking to the universe all your life without even realizing it, and it has been listening to you.
First off, just remember the universe is a living, conscious being.
Every single time you have a thought in your mind, you just spoke to the universe.
Every single time you make an action, you spoke to the universe.
Every single time you judge someone, you just spoke to the universe.
Every single time you just made one decision over the other. You spoke to the universe
The universe has just been taking everything you've been saying in and reflecting it back to your life.
So the life that you see around you right now, you literally called it, you are the one that created it. So talking to the universe is not just when you're meditating and you're praying.
It's actually ALL the time!

– @spirituallyalign

Introduction

> *Every day is another chance to change your life through consciousness.*
>
> — *Steven Ernest Morrow*

ALL YOUR DREAMS AND DESIRES FULFILLED ... Are you ready?

There are actionable steps you can take to shift and change your life through consciousness, helping you create a better and more magnificent you!

Most of us don't know much about our consciousness —our awareness of internal processes within and without us and how our thoughts, feelings, and actions affect our own personal universe. This is by design. We are in school on this Earth.

Choosing to develop your consciousness in a positive way is your direct connection to living a more magical reality and one of the greatest gifts you can give yourself. I know this because everything I've experienced—good, bad, and the infinite in-between—is a direct result of how I've developed my consciousness.

Why I'm Sharing My Journey with You

> *When you arise in the morning, think of what precious privilege it is to be alive, to breathe, to think, to enjoy, to love.*
>
> — Marcus Aurelius

My primary intention in sharing my story with you is to offer a gentle (or maybe not so gentle) reminder of your magnificence. Living in the most magnificent way you can is the loftiest goal that you came here to obtain, and choosing to develop your consciousness in a positive way is how you can do that.

Living Proof

> *Each new day is a blessing, let go of all worries and be grateful for all the positive in your life.*
>
> — @buddhaquotes__

Over the years, I've experienced firsthand how developing my consciousness has transformed not just how I feel, but how the world has responded to me. As I kept my gaze firmly focused on Seeking the Kingdom—engaging in practices that help me turn inward and connect with God —not only did my thoughts and choices change, but my circumstances did as well. Doors opened for me that human logic simply cannot explain. Back in 2002, I started a company that worked with charities all over the United States. Over the next twelve years, that company raised over five-and-a-half million dollars for meaningful causes and helped a lot of people.

When I sold that business, I did not have a master plan, but I did have my spiritual practices, which encouraged me to listen to that voice within. That voice guided me toward an investment that multiplied beyond what I had ever imagined!

Every time I chose to listen inwardly instead of chase outwardly, the Universe opened new doors for me. My house in Colorado sold in perfect timing to a record profit that was unprecedented for properties in the area. My realtor commented, "You sold at a time where there was a two-week high, at a price that had never been that high and might never be again." In fact, the house resold two years later at a $180,000 loss!

My business ventures multiplied with ease, and so many moments of unexpected grace happened that reminded me that I'm always supported. I share these experiences not to boast but to demonstrate what becomes possible when you choose to live in God-consciousness, the place where you fully trust that God wants you to be loving, happy, healthy, wealthy, and wise, instead of relying on human ego and trying to control everything yourself (living in *human-consciousness*).

I am living proof that this is possible for you too.

So if you dream of a life that is full of miracles, one where you have the power to create all your dreams and desires, then this book was put in your hands for a reason.

Finding Your Own Words for God

> *Put your mind on God and begin to let the possibilities bubble up.*
>
> — Dr. Roger Teel

Throughout this book, I use terms such as God, the Universe, and Spirit. I realize these words can carry a lot of cultural weight, history, and even trauma for many of us. If you find that any of these terms don't resonate with you, please feel free to insert your own words based on your beliefs and experiences. If you feel resistance to a word, you can interchange it with whatever is most energetically resonant with your being.

It may be Energy, Nature, the Creator, or another term that feels most comfortable in your heart. What matters isn't the word, *it's the feeling of something greater than ourselves.*

This life force is in and all around us. It makes up the fabric of everything seen and unseen.

You can tap into this force by Seeking the Kingdom, and there are many ways to do this. Reading self-help books, attending seminars, seeking out inspiring teachers —these can all be part of your personal journey to Seek the Kingdom (more on this later). However, the most vital practice for Seeking the Kingdom is turning inward through meditation.

Meditation has been an extraordinarily powerful method of turning inward in my life. In Chapter 4, *The Practice of Meditation*, I'll share my personal practice and provide practical steps so you can start your own path toward turning within—shifting and molding your consciousness and creating a beautiful, vibrant, magical, and meaningful life.

Shifting Our Consciousness: The Framework

> *Life is a mirror and will reflect back to the thinker what he thinks into it.*
>
> — Ernest Holmes

This book is guided by one central principle: You can improve your life simply by shifting your consciousness. Let's briefly walk through the chapters to give you a preview of how each part builds on this transformative idea.

Chapter 1, *Change Your Consciousness, Change Your Life*, defines what consciousness really is. I will share my life story—the highs and the lows—to show you how this all works in real life.

Chapter 2 explores one of the core philosophies behind this framework: *Whatever Happens to You Happens Through You*. I'll expand on this idea and connect it to God-consciousness versus human-consciousness.

Chapter 3, *A Having-Consciousness: The Abundance Mindset*, brings everything into the physical realm. I'll guide you through developing an abundance mindset, with tips on growing and maintaining your *having-consciousness.*

Chapter 4, *The Benefits of Meditation*, takes a deep dive into meditation—its benefits and how to practice it —and other ways to Seek the Kingdom.

Chapters 5 and 6, *The Divine Plan* and *The Reincarnation Cycle*, bring us into more profound spiritual territory. I'll share my thoughts on predestiny, reincarnation, and soul contracts, along with lessons from my own life that can help you live more authentically.

Finally, Chapter 7, *The Mind-Body Relationship*, ties it all together with practical ways to change your habits and improve your physical health.

You were NOT born to be unhappy, sick, broke, alone, or miserable, though at times you may believe this, for it might have been this way for what seems like forever. You were born to be happy, healthy, abundant, vibrant, and surrounded by loving relationships.

It's not in my nature to tell anyone what they should do. I only wish to share the lessons I've experienced while walking my path because when you develop your consciousness to reflect your innermost self, life becomes magical! You become the person you were always meant to be.

The ideas in this book are more than words on a page; they are a way of living—a way of creating a life you want with the people, feelings, opportunities, and abundance you've always dreamed of having.

This book will find itself in the hands of anyone ready to shift their consciousness and profoundly change their life. If you're reading this, I know it will help you create your own magical life.

Are you ready to start your journey? Let's begin.

Chapter One

Change Your Consciousness, Change Your Life

> *Mindset is everything. The difference between a good day and a bad day is your attitude. Your mind is a powerful thing. When you fill it with positive thoughts, your life will start to change. Consciousness is the state of being aware of and responsive to one's surroundings. To shift your life, you must first shift your mindset. Believe you can and you're halfway there.*
>
> — @conscious_soulll

From a young age I have been developing my consciousness (perhaps you have been too), and yet it wasn't until I was in my sixties that I truly began to grasp and understand its meaning and how it can improve our lives if we develop it properly.

Your consciousness is what you really, deeply believe about yourself and the world, and thus informs what you see in and around you every day.

My consciousness has always been vital to creating the abundant life I desire. I will share my strategies on how you can shift your consciousness and bring all the dreams and desires you have ever wanted into reality.

You Hold the Power

When you start to understand that everything that manifests in your life directly results from your thoughts and feelings, you begin to see that everything you allow into your life is, in some way, a choice you've made. It occurs through you and is not merely a matter of good or bad luck. Yes, sometimes hard circumstances can continuously arrive in our lives, but you always have a choice in how to respond. You can choose to respond from a vibration of fear or from a vibration of love (vibration being the inner state or energy you're operating from). These subtle vibrational choices allow you to see calamity as an adventure, loss as space for something new, and sickness as an opportunity for rest if you accept the invitation to listen, even in the worst of times.

So many variables of our fortune are out of our hands,

and yet, so many are within our hands. If you start bringing the variables you can control into your awareness, you will see that there is less luck to this life than you may have supposed.

You can blame others and situations for what is happening in your life, but when you do this, you give away your ability to create change. Change is an inside job, and by taking ownership of every part of your present moment—words, thoughts, feelings, sensations, and reactions—you recover your ability to create wonderful lasting change in your life. Blame is an explanation and analysis of the past, but your opportunity to make lasting change comes from the present. And while you have every right to blame people, circumstances, and even God for the past, it won't do anything but cause you misery. By giving up blame, you can start creating the life you've always dreamed of, from the present moment.

So What Does Holding the Power Look Like?

It means that you understand a powerful truth: Your life, circumstances, ups, and downs aren't events happening ***to you***, and they aren't occurring just to make you miserable.

When you believe life is circumstantial and happens to you, it may feel like you are at the mercy of life. You might even feel like a pawn in some random game of chess that you don't understand.

This can make you feel like nothing you say or do will make a difference, which can cause feelings of hopelessness. You might feel like life keeps coming at you in all the wrong ways. You might feel like you're not in charge of your own life, or that it's not working at all in your favor.

Holding the power means understanding that you can decide at any given moment to awaken to the realization that you want a better life, and that you actually have the power to do something about it. That allows you to turn all the dreams and desires you've been longing for into your actual reality.

You are the sum total of what you have been bringing into your life since Day One, the day you came into existence. It's all part of what helps you grow into the person (and soul) you are meant to be. And don't forget, life is all about choices and you have the ability to choose and create greatness within yourself right now.

Two Things You Can Do Today to Become a Cocreator of Your Own Life

In my humble opinion, the most powerful and rewarding thing you can do to become a cocreator of your own life is to pause several times a day, get quiet in your meditations, and become aware of all the marvelous blessings unfolding around you in remarkable ways. Subconsciously, a great deal of your attention might begin to focus on what you don't like, so taking the opportunity to actively notice how much good is present around you will allow you to begin noticing and enhancing these blessings.

A second wondrous thing you can do is to practice gratitude for each blessing that comes your way. When you learn how to express gratitude and truly enter the soft vibratory state of giving thanks for all the blessings that you're surrounded by daily, more and more bountiful blessings will continue to appear. I will explore the practice of gratitude in Chapter 3.

Shifting Perspectives

> *But seek ye first the kingdom of God, and his righteousness; and all these things shall be added unto you.*
>
> — Matthew 6:33

I'd like to offer some concrete and significant ideas to help you realize and achieve this new mindset, one which offers you choices.

You're at a crossroads. You're feeling stagnant or stuck, and you have a choice: Continue as you always have or forge a brand new path. If at this point you are starting to feel like there may be more to life than what you have experienced so far, let me tell you about this new path. On it, miracles happen frequently and amazing manifestations are available not only to you, but to all living beings.

God gave everyone the same unique ability to connect to Him, no matter their circumstances. Whether you're reading this book in a mansion, in an office, in a prison, under a bridge, or anywhere in between, God's line of communication is open to you. Connecting to God (or your personal higher Source) is a choice we can make each day.

God has given us simple ways to connect. We all have the ability to Seek the Kingdom in whatever form we choose. The easiest and most accessible way (my personal favorite) is through a daily meditation practice. I'll expand on this in Chapter 4.

Reading spiritual books (such as this one) is another way. You can also opt to attend self-help seminars or even seek out a teacher or a guru if those options are available to you. Once you start Seeking the Kingdom and connecting to God, believe me, your life will begin to transform. Spiritual practices will allow you to recognize the miracles that are already in your life, and will help you open up to the increasing flow of possibilities that will begin to make its way toward you. Once these miracles start to unfold, your job will simply be to receive them with gratitude—the vibrational state that allows you to receive and is essential if you want your miracles to continue multiplying.

No matter what's happening in our lives, each of us can take the time to connect to God every day.

How do you know this can work for you? Well, let me tell you how this unfolded for me in my own life—how I realized the role my consciousness was playing, how I befriended it, and how I grew from it—and how my life flourished for many, many years as a result.

My Story

In my early twenties, I got married. My father had married at twenty-one, so I was excited to be starting a life with a woman I loved deeply at the time at around the same age he did. I was young, naive, and excited about the future, deeply believing I was doing what I was supposed to do.

At the tender age of twenty-two, it felt as though life itself began to shudder and shake. Less than six months after saying "*I do,*" my wife's father passed away, and to my utter surprise, my wife said, "*I need to be alone and grieve.*" This stunned me, mostly because I hold the belief that people typically want to be surrounded by loved ones when they are hurting. Yet, wanting to be a supportive husband, I trusted my wife to grieve in the way most suitable for her own soul's healing.

This wasn't easy, as I had recently purchased the condominium where we were living, and she was essentially asking me to leave my own home. But for the sake of her healing, I respected her request and slept on my best friend's couch.

At first, I thought she would need a day or two, perhaps a week at most. But weeks drifted by and the next thing I knew, I had stayed away from my home for two months.

Before any of this had happened, I had been planning to handle some minor household repairs that I had put off for some time. So one day, when I knew she would be at work, I took the opportunity to go back to the condo during my lunch break to inspect what I might need to do later.

When I entered the house, my eyes were drawn immediately to a card standing on the kitchen table. I paused, simply looking at it, and my curiosity got the better of me. I held the card in my hand and was hit with the immediate realization that this was a romantic card. It had come from someone who I believed was engaged in a sexual relationship with my wife. My breath left my body, and I was gripped with a kind of pain I had never felt before.

Not knowing what I was doing, I ran out of the house in my suit pants and dress shoes and continued running and running. The pain was overwhelming my mind, and I had no idea how far I was running or where I was going, but I sensed it was quite a distance. The next day, I couldn't even get out of bed because my muscles were beyond exhausted. This muscle fatigue lasted a couple of days. I realized my mind had driven my body farther than it probably should have to escape from the pain vibrating through it.

I later calculated the length of my run and it was several miles, in my dress shoes. No wonder I was sore and exhausted and couldn't walk for two days.

My heart ached, my head spun, and the days felt like a blur. I can't remember how I made it through that time.

My wife and I attempted reconciliation, but after five months, I still couldn't get the image of her infidelity out of my head. I realized I could no longer remain in the marriage; I could not rebuild the broken trust between us.

Once I took the opportunity to step back after the initial anguish had dissipated, I started to see the silver lining. One of the blessings I received from this painful time still serves me now (and will continue to serve me for the rest of my life): the ability to see painful experiences as an opportunity to grow.

The pain of this traumatic period slowly healed with time. Today, it feels far away and long gone. I hardly think about it. I thank God for getting me through that harrowing period of my life, for healing me, and for making me all the better for it.

At the Crossroads

I can clearly see two paths I potentially could have taken during this difficult time. I might have (justifiably) stayed entrenched in bitterness and discontent, but I chose a different path, a more liberating path—my path.

I had been attending church since childhood, and reading about personal growth and spirituality since I was eighteen. But this overwhelming, deep, heartfelt pain drove me to go even deeper into my spiritual journey. I might have chosen to look outward and numb the pain of betrayal in innumerable unhealthy ways. Instead, l dove deeper inward into my spiritual practices.

The choice I made—looking inward and Seeking the Kingdom—is what has made the journey that has followed so miraculous.

As I searched for healing through books and seminars, one practice kept appearing again and again, commanding my attention: meditation. The common denominator I kept hearing over and over was to "Meditate!" Yet despite all my spiritual seeking, I had never actually tried it.

I knew the extended pain and anxiety weren't physically healthy for me, and there had to be a different route through it. With that in mind, I started studying any and all resources on meditation I could find, and finally, I said to myself,

"It's time. I'm going to give it a try."

I chose to meditate for the first time. I knew nothing about meditation, so I sat down on a hard wooden chair in my dining room and closed my eyes, and with that began what has become a lifelong meditation journey. I can't imagine what my life might have been like had I not started.

The Journey into Stillness

Draw a line in the sand, and God will be there every step of the way on your meditation journey.

On my quest to improve my meditation practice, I kept hearing: *"Be still and clear your mind. Don't ask for anything, just allow God to be present in the silence."*

This wasn't easy. I had so many thoughts racing around in my head, but somehow, over time, I learned to quiet my mind or at least be silent in segments, and I began to experience some space between my thoughts.

What I found was that my thoughts continuously attempted to interrupt the stillness and that it's my job as a meditator to lovingly push them away in order to expand the stillness.

Even after forty-five years of meditation, thoughts still come and go. But years of practice has taught me to more easily return to the silence of my center and my inner peace each time.

This practice changed my life in miraculous ways.

The Epiphany

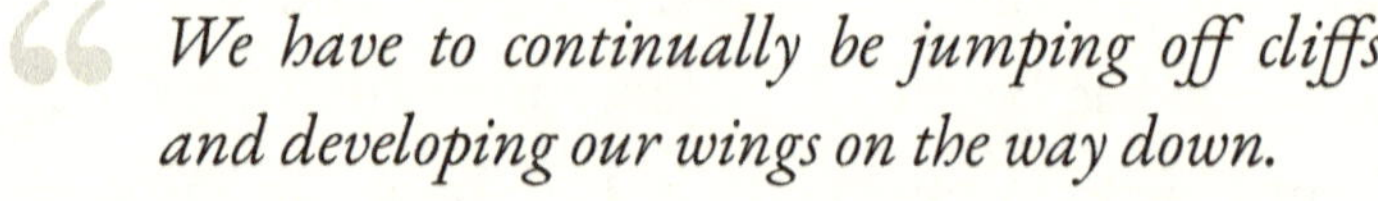

> *We have to continually be jumping off cliffs and developing our wings on the way down.*
>
> — Unkonown Author

And then, an epiphany happened in my life!

Two weeks into my meditation practice, not really knowing if I was doing it correctly, I found myself looking for guidance. I was pleasantly surprised when I ran across a notice at my church in Colorado telling of a meditation retreat being offered in Grand Teton National Park in Wyoming, about a nine-hour drive from where I lived.

I was looking to improve my meditation, and suddenly here was an opportunity to go deeper!

The retreat was to be held at the Jackson Lake Lodge, surrounded by rustic retreat cabins. I was intrigued. I took a leap of faith and signed up, not knowing what the experience had in store for me.

On the first day of the retreat, I arrived at the check-in desk, where I met a man with whom I immediately felt incredibly comfortable. What I didn't know then was that this connection would, in time, wholly and utterly transform my life.

The first session was in the evening, and being a shy twenty-three-year-old in a large group composed of a largely older demographic, I chose a seat in the back. I remember a large table piled with books for sale in the back of the hall. After sitting down, I turned around and saw the same man I had met at the check-in desk: Reverend Al Heard.

Reverend Heard and I nodded at each other and a warm feeling flowed through my body. Sitting beside him was Lady Betty, his assistant. For some reason, later on that evening, I was drawn to look back once more in this man's direction. However, he wasn't there. Something in me pushed me to get up and walk toward Lady Betty, who had been sitting next to him. I asked her where he had gone. She responded that he wasn't feeling well and had left to rest in his room. Without thinking, I left the conference to go find him and see if he needed anything. As I approached his room, I saw him in the doorway of his cabin and asked, "*How are you feeling?*"

To my surprise, he said with his arms stretched wide, *"I'm feeling better now that you're here!"*

In that moment, I felt like his godly essence was connecting with my godly essence—a genuine soul connection. This left me feeling truly accepted and loved.

This was the deepest and most instantaneous connection I've ever experienced to date. I felt so warmed by this complete stranger's presence. It was as though he was not a stranger at all. Something about our soul-deep connection told me he was meant to be my mentor. Meeting him and learning more about meditation has left me feeling empowered, emboldened, and energized.

So much so that by the time I returned to Colorado, I had slipped into a certain quality of feeling, crossing over into what I think was actually another dimension while still currently attached to this earthly dimension.

Even now, all these years later, I find it hard to describe. It was the most profound and incredible feeling I could possibly dream of or desire—pure bliss!

It was a euphoria unlike anything I'd known. I felt all my worldly desires slip away. I was without a care in the world. The things I'd been so desperately wanting lost their attraction. I didn't care about material possessions and nice things like cars, houses, fancy clothing, or anything materialistic—I just had the feeling of being totally present, in God, in the here and now.

The contentment I felt went beyond the normalities of life—a deep calm and happiness I could feel in my whole body. But this wasn't happiness that came from getting what I wanted or having my needs met. Most of us are happy when we know we'll have housing next week, when our bank account looks good, when life is going smoothly. But this joy had nothing to do with ANY of that! It simply was. I was just happy. Deeply, profoundly, inexplicably HAPPY. I was experiencing the grace of God within me.

It was like going to a heavenly place—the heaven

described in the Bible and many holy books—but without dying.

I was still on this plane but in a much more serene mental and emotional space than I had ever experienced before. Once I had crossed over into this place, there wasn't anything else I wanted other than to deepen my connection with God through my spirituality.

I still don't know why I entered that euphoric state of being at such a young age, but I suspect it was to help me grow in ways I hadn't considered, and to let me know it's possible to live on this earthly plane while being in a heavenly state of mind and being. That time period has been one of the best of my entire life. I've been fortunate to have experienced many profound things in my lifetime, but nothing quite compares to being in that blissful state.

While I don't know why I received this gift, I'm so eternally grateful for that euphoric life-changing experience.

My Next Chapter

I remember trying to explain my spiritual experiences to my coworkers. I talked about how I felt inspired to quit my job—I was the manager of a Nautilus health club in Colorado at the time—to go deeper into my spiritual journey. They looked at me like I was crazy for wanting to give up such a lucrative and stable job with no plans, no savings, and no other job lined up!

But I knew in my heart what felt right. I wanted to be near to, and learn from, Reverend Heard. The Reverend served as a minister at the Centers for Spiritual Living (formerly the Religious Science Church) in Salt Lake City, so I quit my job in Denver and applied to health clubs in Utah. I was offered a job as a salesperson, a demotion from my previous managerial position. This is something that previously would have bummed me out, but something dramatic had shifted in me after the retreat, and I didn't care at all about the demotion. I accepted the job, sold my condo, packed all my belongings into my truck and camper, and drove to Utah.

At the retreat, Reverend Heard had introduced me to a young married couple around my age, both in their early twenties. Before I headed out to Salt Lake City, the wife asked her parents if they would have room for me to stay in their house until I got settled. They graciously said yes, but the only space they had was the living room floor, in a sleeping bag. I was so at peace within myself, I didn't care where I slept.

Deep in my being I knew this to be the next step on my journey to personal growth and development. I was excited to see what the future held for me.

I got the sense that I had spent many years searching for a being like the Reverend, someone to guide me. We developed a deep relationship in the form of mentorship, student-teacher, and friendship despite an age gap of forty-plus years between us. He was sixty-five, and I was only twenty-three, but to this day, I've never felt so connected to another human being. Life has a funny way of showing us exactly what we need, when we need it.

Reverend Heard and I had a friendship beyond what I've ever known or dreamed of having with another person. No one could believe we'd only known one another for a few weeks.

My intention was to spend the next two years studying and growing with Reverend Heard and another four years to become a licensed minister, but God had other plans.

The Universe Provides

I was basking in deep gratitude for the opportunity to be studying with Reverend Heard when something miraculous happened.

The company I worked for owned two health clubs. When I first started there as a salesperson, each club had its own manager who had been running things for several years. But a few months into my job, the company made a shocking move—they fired both managers and promoted me to general manager overseeing both clubs! I was in shock. I had not asked either the company or the Universe for this gift. I had simply been showing up, doing my work, and enjoying my spiritual studies with Reverend Heard while deepening my meditation practice.

In my new role, I was responsible for marketing, managing operations, and growing the company's profits. The club offered me $50,000 a year plus bonuses based on performance—and believe me, that was serious money in the early 1980s! They even gave me a fancy little company sports car.

With my newfound money, I bought a gorgeous condo and adorned it with exquisite furnishings. These were things I'd only dreamed of having. But after moving away from the only home I ever knew, crashing on the floor of a stranger's home in a sleeping bag, and working as a salesperson, the Universe had now given me a sports car, a lovely condo, and the opportunity to manage two athletic clubs.

During all of this, I remained in this serene, euphoric space. My meditations had opened pathways for me to stay in the flow of life. That's when it hit me: When you get quiet and still, more will come to you than you can possibly imagine. Your dreams and desires start to come true, like magic. But it's not magic—it's God in action! All you have to do is Seek the Kingdom.

I can't stress this enough: Meditation isn't about asking for or receiving things—it's about communing with God. Our journey on this planet is to always remember to Seek the Kingdom first and foremost.

Simply seeking communion with God through your meditations will bring you into the present and the flow, where gratitude, abundance, and miracles exist. More on this in Chapter 3.

When I was living in that euphoric state, I struggled to put it into words. For years, I had no language for what had happened to me until I ran across Indian spiritual teacher, yogi, and author Sadhguru's message on Instagram about the "Agna." Something clicked! The Agna is a chakra, or energy center, located between the eyebrows, also known as the third eye. Chakras are centers in your body where different energy pathways come together, and the Agna is connected to clarity and seeing things exactly as they are. When this chakra is strong, some people see things so clearly they lose interest in all material concerns. That was what I had experienced when I crossed into this euphoric state. I looked at everything with complete clarity, and all the things I thought mattered no longer mattered at all.

Maybe it was a gift earned from moving through life and doing the inner work. Maybe the inner work pushed my awareness past my ego and into a new space, an alternate state of consciousness, a higher level of evolution. Whatever the reason, I found myself in a state of mystic transcendence, and I was able to maintain it for around six months to a year.

In this alternate state of consciousness, I transcended want.

The EGO—Edging God Out

Time went by in my new life in Salt Lake City, and I began once more to identify with all the trappings of life and my EGO—a process I call "Edging God Out." For some reason, the incredible, euphoric, spiritual life wasn't good enough for me anymore. I had gotten used to it and begun taking all the abundance I was experiencing for granted, and it no longer felt magical.

The EGO process began moving me out of this euphoric place, and my ego began to run the show once more. Once that started happening, I began to actively fulfill my ego's desires, and I found myself wanting more and more!

As my egoic identification began to take over, I made two regrettable changes in my life.

First, I decided that the fancy little company sports car wasn't enough; it was used, and used wasn't cool. So, I went out and got the top-of-the-line Saab Turbo sports car (one of the nicest available at the time) and drove it off the showroom floor.

The second change I made was deciding to find an

individual investor so I could start my own health club. Managing other people's clubs wasn't enough for me anymore. I wanted to start my own.

Why shouldn't I? Both the health clubs I was managing had transformed from nearly closing their doors to successful, vibrant businesses. I was seeing abundant financial success and was essentially managing the entire company. I was even asked by Reverend Heard to start a program called "Create Financial Success in Your Life," designed for a crowd much older than myself.

On top of all that, I began dating a woman who was drop-dead gorgeous, filling the void and sense of lack left in me after the drama of my divorce and previous marriage.

Looking back, I realize I started to believe it was me who had created all the success I was enjoying—that *I* was the one who knew what to do and how to do it. I had worked hard, yes, but the real issue was that I had stopped honoring and being grateful for how God had been guiding and supporting me. I started giving my ego all the credit instead.

I fell into the belief that all these trappings were somehow a result of how smart, accomplished, and hard-working I was. I bequeathed all the success to myself.

I was forgetting that it wasn't through ego that I manifested all these opportunities and gifts—it was through Seeking the Kingdom. It was around this time that I stopped Seeking the Kingdom altogether, thinking it was no longer needed.

But life will always treat you the way you treat it. Not long after making these changes to my life, my streak of success started to run out and things quickly went downhill.

My new business partner and I found a vacant building in an ideal location to start our new health club. We began offering presale memberships at a steep discount; if people signed up before we opened, they could lock in long-term contracts at 75 percent off. The response was great! Many clients signed up and made down payments, and we were quickly raising money.

After a couple of months, my partner bailed on the entire project. He told me he was done and that he would be keeping all the money we had raised!

He didn't even plan to return any of the money to clients who had made a down payment on a membership.

Thankfully, when the Attorney General's office got involved due to the level of fraud that had taken place, they realized that twenty-four-year-old me wasn't the one behind the scheme and set out to prosecute my ex-business partner instead.

To make matters worse, the owners of the original clubs I was managing figured out I had been working silently toward creating competition for them behind their backs and ended up firing me.

This, in turn, led me to complete a "deed in lieu of foreclosure" on my luxurious condo. To cover the legal costs for the deed without sufficient personal finances, I had to give my attorney all my high-end furniture.

Ultimately, I lost my home, luxury furniture, fancy car, and the lifestyle I'd become accustomed to living.

Not only did I lose everything I had gained, but I had also lost the most meaningful relationship I have ever had.

My minister, mentor, and best friend, Reverend Al Heard, passed away.

The Reverend's Passing

The Reverend died on a Sunday.

This particular day, the church enjoyed the largest congregation of any other Sunday. One hundred twenty-five people attended the Reverend's sermon that morning. I remember him delivering an especially touching speech. Later on, we participated in an evening of square dancing, and at about 10 p.m., the crowd dispersed, and everybody, including the Reverend, made their way home.

Things changed quickly at around midnight when I received a call from Lady Betty who said that the Reverend wasn't doing well. Something in her voice alarmed me. I threw on some clothes and sped across town to the Reverend's house at 90 miles per hour, my heart racing the entire way.

When I arrived, I saw police cars and an ambulance surrounding the property. My stomach dropped. I rushed up to the front door and asked one of the officers how the Reverend was doing.

He looked at me and said quietly, "I'm sorry. He's passed."

Over the two years we'd spent together, Reverend Heard would often turn to me with a smile and say, "Hey Buddy," in the most soothing way. It was his greeting, his way of showing love—something he'd say during our weekly dinners, at church, or driving around town together.

When I entered the room where his body lay, I sat down on his bed and held his hand. For half an hour, I looked at him and whispered, "Hey Buddy ... Hey Buddy ... Hey Buddy ..."

The Reverend was a man of great kindness and humility, someone who always found a way to give people exactly what they needed at that moment. He prioritized peace over being right, and his loving presence could bring calm to any situation. I witnessed this countless times, but one story stands out in particular.

The church rented its space from a private owner. The congregation wanted to create a nativity scene one Christmas and had agreed with the owner of the space and the cleaning team that no bales of hay would be brought into the church. Yet, somebody had brought in hay and had left a large mess. When a woman arrived to clean up, she started yelling and fretting about the agreement. She was terribly upset, and even though she wasn't saying nice things to the Reverend, he went up to her and gave her the biggest hug, apologizing and thanking her for being there to help with the cleanup.

He has remained in my heart ever since, and he always will.

Everything I've shared with you so far—my journey with meditation, the miracles that showed up, learning from my mistake of putting my ego first, my time with the Reverend—are all events that led to miraculous realizations because I chose to develop my consciousness.

Now it's time to delve into understanding what consciousness is and how you can work with it to create your own magical life.

Chapter Two

Whatever Happens to You Happens Through You

> *No matter what the lips may be saying, the inner thought outspeaks them and the unspoken work often carries more weight than the spoken ... What you are speaks so loudly that I cannot hear what you say.*
>
> — Ernest Holmes

Taking steps to shift your consciousness by learning how to shift your thoughts is the first stage in creating your unique destiny.

This puts **you** in charge of your circumstances and outcomes. There's no need to blame others or even God if things aren't going as planned, because you have the power to change it!

Your consciousness is constantly creating your experience based on what you've been feeding it throughout your entire life. What feeds your consciousness? Your thoughts, feelings, words, and actions—every single day. Whatever happens to you is happening through you, shaped by the consciousness you've been developing all along.

From Human-Consciousness to God-Consciousness

> *Work with your consciousness until it ceases to function on the level of problem and begins to function on the level of answer.*
>
> — Ernest Holmes

While Jesus, Confucius, Lao Tzu, Muhammad, Buddha, and other spiritual luminaries/enlightened masters lived in God-consciousness constantly, most of us move between human-consciousness and God-consciousness throughout our lives. The goal is to always progress—to spend more time in God-consciousness and less in human-consciousness as you go through life. Each moment you choose to seek God through meditation, prayer, and spiritual study, you strengthen your ability to remain in God-consciousness.

Taking actions to shift your consciousness creates changes that can alter your life in wonderful and miraculous ways. The methods outlined in this book will help you shift from human-consciousness to God-consciousness.

When you remain in human-consciousness, life becomes limited and you have to struggle and grab at everything you need or want. You might only experience a small portion of all the good that is actually available to you in your life journey. All you dream of and desire come very, very slowly, or might never even happen at all. Everything feels like a battle, requiring a lot of effort. That is how a lot of people choose to experience life.

When you're living in God-consciousness, miraculous opportunities manifest. Your dreams simply begin to show up in grand, unexpected ways. When you explore and change your consciousness, you will be able to make space for more blessings to enter your life, and be more profoundly present and involved in everything you do.

Manifesting your desired life from human-consciousness is painstakingly slow, while it feels rapid and almost natural when you're in God-consciousness. I've always chosen to pursue God-consciousness, and I have always experienced my life as magical!

No matter your age or where you are on your humanly journey, you can always choose to start walking in the beautiful path of God-consciousness

Developing Our Consciousness

There are as many personalities as there are people on this planet. From my perspective, the only thing that separates one from the other is how they've developed their consciousness.

My own journey with consciousness has led me to a knowing that God has always been guiding me and will always continue to guide my way toward happiness, as long as I continue to turn inward every day and prioritize Seeking the Kingdom in my life.

Seeking the Kingdom regularly through meditation and other spiritual practices means you are actively choosing to live in God-consciousness, not to ask for things but simply for the joy of communing with God.

All of us have our own unique connection to the Universe. That means it is listening to you through all the thoughts you believe in your mind, the emotions you feel, the words you say (and don't say), and the things you do (or don't do). That constitutes your consciousness, and you're building it one day at a time.

All your life's circumstances—both good and bad—can help you grow and push you along the path to a greater and more fulfilled life, but only if you learn how to always be aware of what you are thinking, feeling, saying, and doing.

I cannot stress enough that Seeking the Kingdom is the most powerful and profound thing you'll ever do for your life.

The Nature of Consciousness

It's a question that has been pondered by philosophers, scientists, and seekers from all walks of life for centuries. Consciousness is defined by *Merriam-Webster* dictionary as *"the quality or state of being aware especially of something within oneself [...] the state of being characterized by sensation, emotion, volition, and thought,"*[1] but what exactly does this mean?

Well, I'd like to propose two perspectives/methods in exploring and understanding consciousness: subjective and inward-facing, and scientific and outward-facing.

The Subjective Perspective

The first is the *subjective perspective*, where consciousness is understood as an **inner experience.** It's the part of you that observes your surroundings and feelings, and makes meaning out of everything that happens in your life. Practices like meditation or quiet reflection are powerful tools to view and study this inner world and see how your thoughts and feelings shape what you experience.

From this vantage point, consciousness is unique to the individual. It is all about the individual's experience of the world and how they interpret and understand it. You have been interpreting the world and developing your consciousness your entire life.

This is where an eye-opening truth begins to reveal itself: Whatever happens to you happens through you. Your subjective consciousness is developed from every-

---

1. *Merriam-Webster.com Dictionary*, s.v. "consciousness," accessed November 6, 2025, https://www.merriam-webster.com/dictionary/consciousness.

thing you think, feel, say, and do. Your experience is filtered through the state of your inner world. Change that inner world, and you begin to change everything around you.

The Scientific Perspective

The second way to look at consciousness is through the *scientific perspective*. This approach studies what's **outside of us**: the physical evidence of what we call awareness. Scientists explore consciousness by studying the brain, the nervous system, and even the vastness of the Universe itself. They search for patterns that explain the nature of consciousness and how it arises.

From this viewpoint, consciousness is seen as a biological and neurological process, as a product of brain activity and measurable data. Science seeks to understand the *mechanics* of consciousness, for example, how neurons fire, how memories form, and how thought translates into actions and behaviors.

While this perspective gives us useful information on the physical aspects of consciousness, it cannot capture what it feels like, or the meaning behind consciousness. It tells us what's happening, but not what it *means*.

That is where the subjective perspective fills in the rest of the story.

What's the Truth?

Well, the truth is that both perspectives make up parts of the whole, and they each offer a unique prism or glance through which you can experience consciousness and how it works. By combining these two perspectives, you can gain a deeper and more nuanced understanding of the nature of consciousness itself.

For the purposes of this book, we will be focusing on the subjective inner experience of consciousness.

But Why Is It Important to Understand Consciousness?

Consciousness is what makes you who you are. Working with and developing awareness around your consciousness can help you to better understand the unique part you are currently playing in the world and provide the opportunity to change, which empowers you to manifest your true dreams and desires.

So, whether you're a philosopher, scientist, or a seeker who's curious about how you fit into this world, learning about consciousness is an incredible journey of inner research.

Your consciousness determines whether you'll live a stagnant life or a magical one. Understanding your consciousness gives you a choice: Be imprisoned by your own thoughts and circumstances, or embark on a journey that takes you to the fulfilling life you truly desire or long for!

When you understand your own consciousness, you have the ability at any moment to get out of harmful repetitive cycles you might be stuck in and change your life for the better.

How Can You Become Aware of Your Consciousness?

One easy way is to examine the fabric of your life: your relationships, activities, clothing, home, job, and even the food you eat.

Are they what you want? Are things going your way?

Are you having a life of love, abundance, health, and spiritual connection, or do you feel stuck in a life that is undesirable?

Whatever your thoughts and feelings are creates who you are.

If things aren't going the way you want, ask yourself:

"What am I thinking?"

"What am I feeling?"

"What am I saying?"

"What am I doing in my life?"

Many people have been wearing a mask to the world for so long, some starting as early as childhood, that they don't even realize that they are disguising their true selves anymore. However, you aren't driven by the layered veneer you expose to the world but rather by your conscious and unconscious mind, deeply seated within you.

Have you ever paid attention to your daily thoughts and feelings or the deeply seated beliefs you hold about yourself and life? If so, then you have engaged in the process of ***introspection***.

What Is Introspection?

Introspection is taking a deep dive into your own mind/thoughts and exploring the inner workings of your consciousness.

Think of introspection as a *window into your psyche, and further, into your soul.* It allows you to observe and understand your own thoughts, emotions, and experiences from the inside out. By practicing introspection, you can gain a deeper understanding of yourself, your beliefs, and the world **you've** created around you.

How Does Introspection Relate to Consciousness?

Introspection is one of the ways that you can access your own consciousness and begin to understand your own true nature and unique perspective.

By tapping into the power of introspection, you can unlock a deeper level of self-awareness and gain insights into your own conscious experience.

So why not take a few moments today to engage in some introspection and start unlocking the power of your own consciousness?

Please remember it's about the real, private things you're saying inside yourself and not the polished outer mask you've been putting on and presenting to the world around you.

Consciousness in Action

The Circle of Giving and Receiving

> *Vibrations don't lie, when you operate at a high frequency, low energies can't touch you. Your frequency is your fortress. Guard it, nurture it. And let it shine.*
>
> — @high.dimention_

The first thing any of us needs to do when we feel we are lacking in any area of life is to shift into the vibrational state of giving. Let me explain what I mean by vibration. It's the space or motivation from which your actions come. It's the energy behind what you do. If you feel lacking, you can take actions to orient yourself toward a more giving vibration.

This intentional practice is not exclusive to monetary gifts (though giving financially is a potent way to attract more financial blessings in your life). You can also share your time, energy, attention, or whatever you can give at the moment, even if it's just a genuine smile!

By giving to others whenever you feel you are lacking, you start the flow of God's natural circle of giving and receiving. By engaging your natural giving nature, for no other reason than to simply give, your life will complete the circle of giving and receiving for **YOU**.

The natural way of human nature is to be a giver. We are mirrors of God, who is the ultimate giver of life—the Source. As we align with the godly vibration of giving and begin to experience this vibrational state, our consciousness shifts to a vibration of abundance. When you are within this vibration, you feel that you have everything you need, and your life begins to mirror this abundance back to you in incredible ways.

Once the circle of giving and receiving is completed, life will start lavishing you in so many unexpected ways.

As an example, to start the giving/receiving flow of money, you can begin by giving even just a small amount. Over time, you will start seeing that you have more and more to give. In my experience, systematic, purposeful giving—10 percent of my monthly budget—has been the single most impactful step I've taken to grow my financial abundance.

By continuously adding more to what you are giving, you will eventually find yourself in the flow of giving and receiving. This will help create your giving–receiving consciousness.

Our Health Is in Our Hands

I run across people who constantly worry about health issues and have not yet been able to take action to change their daily habits. Some worry incessantly about future health issues, but when fear and worry result in endless rumination and stress, it can contribute to an illness actually manifesting. As the saying goes, there's nothing to fear except fear itself.

This same idea is what continually keeps us stuck in unhealthy bodies. When all you can see are the parts of yourself that you do not like, you are not seeing yourself for who you can be: fit, healthy, and sexy. I have met people who say they want to feel healthy but don't move their bodies much or make healthy food choices. They end up getting stuck in a cycle of feeling sluggish and rundown. Maybe someone was an athlete in high school and as an adult still thinks they can continue living the same lifestyle they did back then: eating too much, drinking too much, not getting enough sleep, and stressing out, all the while deluding themselves into thinking that they are healthy.

Here's what I know to be true: If you're developing your God-consciousness by Seeking the Kingdom (primarily through meditation), it puts you in a vibrational space where you naturally make healthier choices. You find yourself wanting to eat healthy, wanting to exercise, wanting to take care of your body. The bad habits lose their grip on you. When you're living in God-consciousness, you cannot help but be happy AND healthy! It's not about forcing yourself through willpower alone or suffering through a diet. It's about shifting the space from which you're making decisions. When you Seek the Kingdom first, everything else, including your health, falls into place.

The Helplessness Mindset

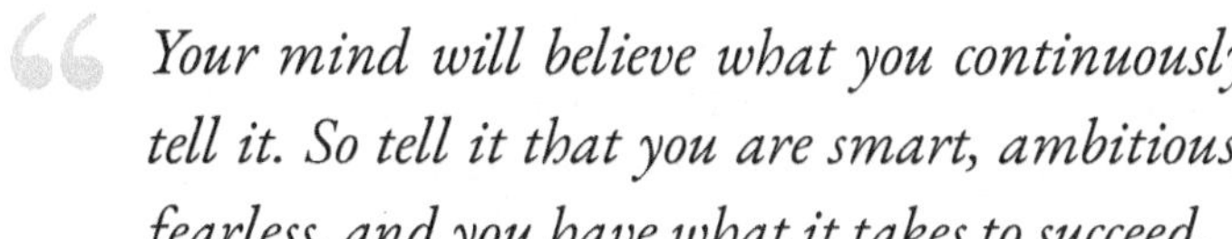

— @spiritualgoal

Another version I have run across is the person who is unhappy but not willing to change.

"*That's just how life is!*" they'll say, throwing up their hands.

I think many people in the world believe God or their circumstances in life are doing something **to** them. I don't think it occurs to them that in spite of the pain and suffering, there are things that are within their control.

In some cases, a person's job, their upbringing, or some other circumstance in their life has caused or is causing them suffering or pain. In cases like this, it is easy to blame external circumstances. But remember, you always have a choice! You may not be able to change the past, but you can change your future. You can choose the vibrational state from which you react and make decisions. You can make decisions from an unhappy or unhealthy consciousness, or you can decide to make decisions from a happy and healthy one.

Things are not happening **to** you, they are happening

through you! If you continue looking at life as a series of things that keep on happening to you, you risk remaining stuck in an unhealthy and unhappy consciousness field. On the contrary, if you shift your mindset and start living in God-consciousness, you start feeling more empowered to make all the changes necessary to live a healthier, happier, more abundant life!

So how do you break free from the helplessness mindset? Seeking the Kingdom and living in God-consciousness is a good way to start.

Remember this: Whatever you think, feel, say, or do becomes you, because whatever happens to you happens through you. You are not a victim of your circumstances. You are a cocreator with God, shaping your reality every single day through your consciousness.

Quick Fixes

I've also run across people who regularly use substances, such as alcohol or drugs, to get by in their lives. Some are pursuing a lifestyle of "I just want to have fun" while others are numbing or distracting themselves from trauma, inner tension, or unhappiness. For some people, the problem might be biological, an issue with the brain's reward pathways.

Whatever the reason, escaping reality through substances is a sign of an unhappy mindset. Viewing your body and your mind as a healthy and happy person will help you make choices that are aligned with that reality!

The Alternative

In contrast, consider this.

I see myself as muscular and fit simply because that is the view I choose to have about myself and *who I want to be*. I choose to have a healthy and happy consciousness, which propels me to make certain lifestyle decisions.

I go to the gym six days a week.

I run or mountain bike daily.

I walk everywhere I can.

I take supplements that help me reach higher levels of wellness.

I eat a clean diet, avoiding junk food and processed foods. I focus on eating whole foods that come from nature.

I drink mostly water; it's another one of the magical elixirs for a happier, healthier life.

It's a priority to me that I do everything I can to stay fit and healthy.

Doctors, clinics, and hospitals are certainly necessary at times, but my goal in life is to stay as healthy as I can using environmental factors within my control, like how I move, what I eat, how I rest, and what supplements I take.

By doing this, I minimize my need to rely on doctors, clinics, and hospitals.

I've developed this relationship with my health over many years, learning what truly works for my body. Through this practice, I've anchored excellent health into my consciousness. **I AM a healthy person**, and my body reflects that truth.

In later chapters I will walk you through the consciousness- and habit-shifting steps that will align your body, environment, and lifestyle with the new way you want to see yourself.

How Can You Create Lasting Change?

> *Today is your opportunity to build the tomorrow you want.*
>
> — Ken Poirot

Well, if you really want to change your life so that you can feel and experience a better YOU, rather than bogging yourself down in more research right away, start creating positive steps in your life now.

What is one step you can take today that will help shift your consciousness **just 1 percent** closer to a healthier, happier you? Approach change **one step at a time**.

Imagine living the life you have always dreamed of, and being the person you have always wanted to be. That is possible, but only if you choose to start shifting your consciousness now. I can promise you there is nothing more satisfying than seeing yourself and your life change thanks to the choices that you make on a daily basis!

Here's the truth: Whatever you've created in your life from the day you were born until now was first developed in your consciousness through every choice you made along the way. And that means each day is an opportunity to build a brand new consciousness and create a brand new reality!

Baby Steps

> *Never leave that till tomorrow which you can do today.*
>
> — Benjamin Franklin

If all this feels overwhelming, start with just one day at a time.

Move more often, take the stairs, walk as many places as you can, spend time in nature, or hit the gym. (Exercise can include all kinds of movement!) Make clean and healthy food choices.

Start today. Then tomorrow. Then the next day.

Change your conscious thoughts and feelings about your own body by living a healthy lifestyle, beginning right now. Don't start "tomorrow" because tomorrow never comes—make yourself a promise and start today!

God has given you a wondrous vessel, and you can either take care of it one day at a time or destroy it one day at a time. The choice is yours! Changing your consciousness doesn't happen overnight, but progress is always about choices. If you desire something different, you need to make different choices. You need to make a shift in your consciousness to move in another direction.

The longer you wait to embrace a healthier lifestyle, the greater the likelihood you'll find yourself imprisoned in an unhealthy body. My wish for you is to avoid that prison entirely—to keep enjoying this precious, God-given experience for as long as possible. So please, don't wait another day. Don't wait until it's too late.

Chapter Three

A Having-Consciousness

> *The greatest gift you can give yourself is a life full of Love, Happiness, Abundance, and Spiritual Nourishment, where your mind is filled with loving thoughts, your heart is overflowing with joy, your financial life is amazing, and your spirit is nourished by the simple pleasures of each and every day.*
>
> — Steven Ernest Morrow

What Is a *Having-Consciousness*?

A *having-consciousness* is a state of mind in which it feels as though you always have more than enough. Within this state, you experience a sense of certainty that whatever you need will be provided for you, exactly when you need it.

A *having-consciousness* isn't about material wealth. It's about how you relate to life itself.

Within your consciousness live mindsets—beliefs and thought patterns that direct your actions and energy. These shape how you view your world and, in turn, how you experience it. While many were inherited from early formative experiences, you have the power to change them, and thus change your own unique universe.

The Abundance Mindset

> “*In our willingness to give that which we seek, we keep the abundance of the universe circulating in our lives.*
>
> — Deepak Chopra

At the core of a *having-consciousness* is the abundance mindset, which is an intentional way of thinking that emphasizes abundance and opportunity rather than scarcity and limitation.

The Power of Abundance

 *Gratitude [...] turns what we have into enough.*

— Melody Beattie

A *having-consciousness* is about embodying an abundance mindset and living from a place of gratitude, generosity, and trust. When you approach your circumstances with a sense of abundance, you are more likely to take risks, pursue your passions, and create opportunities for yourself and others to flourish in every way possible. Actions born from an abundance mindset empower rather than limit you, as your focus is trained on what is possible and not on your limits.

In the state of gratitude and havingness, the risks you take feel more like creative play and less like danger, just like how it might feel to learn a new dance, or use a different type of paint on a canvas. Even starting a new business begins to feel more fun and less daunting. A *having-consciousness* opens you up to possibility.

A key tenet of *having-consciousness* is the recognition of the abundance **already** present in everything around you. In this practice you become aware of all your resources, talents, and relationships, recognizing the myriad ways in which you are currently blessed. When you focus on what you have rather than what you lack, you will begin to see the world as a flowing river of endless opportunities and possibilities.

The thing to remember is that abundance and *having-consciousness* are vibrational spaces that you can embody. They are not things you **buy or acquire.** You become them.

The first step in cultivating a *having-consciousness* is to offer gratitude for what is present in your world; the second step is to be generous with what you have.

When you cultivate a *having-consciousness* through awareness of and gratitude for what is present in your life, you can transform your life in powerful and profound ways, and create a world that is filled with possibility and promise.

Cultivating Gratitude

> *The love we give away is the only love we keep.*
>
> — Elbert Hubbard

Gratitude is a skill, a vibration, and a home that you can rest in during abundant times and times of loss. Learning to be grateful even when you have the bare minimum initiates the process of attracting abundance into your existence.

When you live in the vibrational state of gratitude for

what already exists in your orbit, you make yourself available to attract more abundance, possibilities, and opportunities. This is because gratitude shifts your focus from **what you don't have** to **what you do have**, which in turn helps you see with greater clarity the abundance and multitudes of opportunities in every situation already present in your current path.

If you aren't grateful for what you have today, tomorrow won't be any better or bear more fruit. Being grateful is an attitude that will bring more success and fulfillment into your life. It will open the floodgates of blessings and opportunities.

Hopefully, I have convinced you that a *having-consciousness* is worth cultivating—and within reach. Let's look more closely at the practice of gratitude.

The Practice of Gratitude

Begin to take time each day to reflect on what is currently present in your reality, for this practice is a direct pathway into the present moment from which all creation and abundance are created. This means to simply look at the many blessings you have to be grateful for right now, however simple and common they are, such as the air you breathe freely at this moment, something enjoyable about the place you live, a tree or flower you appreciate walking by, something rewarding about your job, or anything else that might come to mind that's remarkable in your world.

What opportunities are available to you at present?

What possibilities are available to you at present that will move you toward your abundant goals?

Taking time to ponder questions such as these can help you appreciate the ordinary pleasures and see the beauty in the world around you.

Another way to practice gratitude is to simply reach out to your friends and connections and express appreciation for their role in your journey.

I don't think it's possible to show too much gratitude! I express gratitude in every encounter I have with every human being in my world.

Simple Acts of Gratitude

> Gratitude is the wine for the soul: Go on. Get drunk.
>
> — Rumi

You can show gratitude in your texts by adding a "please" or "thank you" to your messages. Use any specific language that feels appreciative **to you**.

You can even use grateful-looking emojis! 😌

When I receive a gift, I take a photo of myself using

that gift and send it to the giver. Receiving a photo from a person I've sent a gift to makes me feel super appreciated, so I make sure to do the same. There's truly no way to go overboard on showing others appreciation, so even if a week or month has passed since you received a gift, don't hesitate to reach out again and share your gratitude.

Gratitude is one of the most powerful tools in your spiritual toolkit. Whether it's sending a thank you note, paying a compliment, or simply being there for someone when they need support, taking the time to show gratitude can help us form stronger, deeper, more loving bonds with others.

I open my meditations each morning by expressing gratitude to each and every treasured being in my life. That's one of many ways to pause and appreciate the gifts already around you.

You might choose to incorporate this into your practice, or if not, you can choose any of the other countless blessings surrounding you to be grateful for.

Cultivating a sense of appreciation for the abundance already present in your life will expand your *having-consciousness* and create space for new abundance and opportunities to flow toward you.

Tracking Gratitude

Let's begin creating your own practice by writing down six things you're grateful for:

1. ______________________________

2. ______________________________

3. ______________________________

4. ______________________________

5. ______________________________

6. ______________________________

I suggest starting a gratitude journal that you can update on a daily basis.

Your gratitude practice will open up space for many new, splendid things to flow into your life. The more aware and appreciative you are of the gifts that begin flowing toward you, the more space you make for new gifts to flow in.

The key is to enter the vibrational space of abundance in order to recognize the gifts that you already have and the ones that are already on their way to you.

Cultivating Generosity

The second foundational practice I use to intentionally cultivate my *having-consciousness* is generosity.

As discussed in previous chapters, by giving freely—money, effort, time, energy, advice, or whatever you can give at the moment—you open yourself up to receiving.

If you feel lonely and lacking in love, share a kind word to someone. If you always feel like you don't have enough time to do anything, intentionally make time to volunteer. If you feel lacking financially, choose to give away a part of your income to people in need on a monthly basis. After all, if you want an orange tree, you have to plant oranges; if you want an oak tree, you have to plant an acorn. Whatever you feel you're lacking, you have to first be generous enough to give it away.

When you approach everything with a spirit of generosity, you create space for more abundance in your life.

> *Give, and it shall be given unto you. A good measure, pressed down, shaken together and running over, will be poured into your lap. For with the measure you use, it will be measured to you.*
>
> — Luke 6:38

Trust the Universe

> *Once you decide you want a good life, the universe will start moving things for you to have it.*
>
> — @universe.guidance

While transitioning from a scarcity to an abundance mindset, your mind will present you with doubts and fears, and to allow the shift to take place in spite of those doubts and fears, you must begin to **trust the Universe**. Choose faith, not fear!

If you are living paycheck to paycheck and are reading about generosity, gratitude, and abundance, it may seem crazy or woo-woo. But believe me, there is real power in trusting that the Universe has your back, and that you are supported as you move toward a *having-consciousness.*

When you let go—and I mean truly let go—of the need to control every aspect of your outcome and trust that everything will work out for the best, that is letting God in.

God's intention and desire for each of us is greatness. When you let go and allow the divine to guide your path, abundant blessings start flowing in. God has perfect timing, but His timing is different from our limited, control-based human timelines, so patience is vital.

By practicing trust in the fact that God always provides, you will learn to relax and flow. When you trust God, you are exactly where you need to be and equipped with everything you need for your next steps!

A *having-consciousness* is about embracing the belief that there is truly enough for everyone. In practice, this looks like loosening your grip on your worries by practicing both gratitude and generosity. The more you lean on these practices, you are training your consciousness to focus on abundance, not lack.

Your days will fill up with opportunities, genuine connections, love, joy, and abundance.

There is a famous story from the Bible (Matthew 14:17-21) that exemplifies a *having-consciousness.*

In this tale, Jesus performs a miracle by multiplying

loaves of bread and fish to feed a large crowd. The story is told in all four Gospels and is considered one of the most famous miracle stories in ancient Judea.

In the tale, Jesus preached to a large crowd of people who had gathered to hear him. As the day went on, the people became hungry and there was no food available to feed them.

Jesus saw their need and asked his disciples to bring forth to him what food they possessed among the disciples, which amounted to a meager five loaves of bread and two fish.

Jesus took the bread and the fish. After thanking God, he began breaking the bread and the fish into pieces, handing them to his disciples to distribute among the large crowd. To the great amazement of everyone, the bread and fish multiplied adequately to feed the entire crowd, said to be in the thousands, with leftover food to spare.

This miracle symbolizes Jesus's compassion, generosity, practice of gratitude, and ability to create beyond what is seen, as well as his power to provide for the needs of others.

It is also seen as a symbol of God's abundance, as it shows that when you trust in God and give everything you have to Him, God can work wonders and provide for your every need.

This story has been interpreted to mean many things based on the level of awareness of the interpreter, but it remains one of the most powerful and inspiring stories in the Bible. Whether or not you identify as a Christian, this story speaks to the importance of compassion, **generosity**, and **faith in God's ability to provide for our needs**.

The lesson I have personally taken from this story is the grand power of gratitude and generosity, even when it seems that I don't have all that I need and want yet.

In this tale, even when Jesus did not possess sufficient food, he used gratitude to enter a state of havingness and abundance—*having-consciousness*—and from within that state, projected abundance outwards, generously providing for others.

Honor and love what you already have, blessing it as Jesus did with the few loaves and fish. What follows will be nothing short of miraculous as you watch it multiply. When our limited human minds cannot see a way, God shows us or creates one for us.

You cannot create abundance by focusing on what you lack, for your focus directs your energy and actions.

If you need further proof of what is freely available to you, please remember that every day you can witness the masterful, inspiring beauty from which all art is derived; the purity of nature that can be experienced when witnessing a sunrise or sunset; and the pragmatic daily applications of human intelligence you benefit from whenever you use technology.

You didn't paint the sunrises and sunsets after years of art school, and yet there they are. You didn't invent the technology that you use, such as TV, cell phones, laptops, iPads, and computers, but they are available for your use.

The opposite of a *having-consciousness* is **one rooted in scarcity.**

In a state of scarcity, the consciousness is focused on what is lacking and holds the belief that there are not enough resources, money, and opportunities for everybody.

The scarcity mindset is often created by trauma or feelings of fear and anxiety rooted in not having enough. In worst cases, this can lead to unhealthy patterns and behaviors, like pathological hoarding stemming from a desire to prepare for all sorts of unrealistic worst-case scenarios, or incessant competition that hampers one's ability to form trusting relationships with others.

When all you can think about are all the ways things can go wrong, you risk missing opportunities to enjoy.

A key trait that will tip you off to your own scarcity mindset is the need for perfectionism and control to the point where it hurts your own mental health. The belief that you can control outcomes of your decisions, the actions of another person, or anything other than your own thoughts, feelings, and actions is rooted in a lack of trust. In scarcity, you might never take action or worry endlessly about the outcomes of an action because you don't have faith that the Universe and God are conspiring in your favor.

Why Is the Scarcity Mindset So Prevalent?

Upbringing

Our childhood social conditioning, as well as cultural factors, may play a role in our scarcity mindset.

Many of us grow up in environments where scarcity is the norm, where resources are limited, and where competition for those resources is high. In such environments, it is natural to internalize the belief that there is not enough to go around and that you must always fight to get your fair share.

In other households with access to great wealth and abundance, cultural factors can play a role in shaping consciousness. In societies that emphasize material success and accumulation, it can be easy to adopt a scarcity mindset, believing that you must accumulate as much wealth and material possessions as possible to be happy or successful.

Media and Advertising

This mindset can be reinforced by messages in the media and advertising, which often promote the idea that you need more in order to be fulfilled. Advertisements are constantly telling all of us we're incomplete without the latest product, the newest upgrade, or the next big thing.

Whether you have a great abundance of material wealth or very little, by focusing on gratitude and creating a *having-consciousness*, you allow yourself to enjoy what you have, making space for new gifts to arrive and giving back what you don't truly need to those who are in greater need.

Challenging Circumstances

> *Power of the tongue is so real. Stop saying you are tired all the time, you're broke or depressed. Start saying you're grateful, start manifesting growth, start speaking life into yourself.*
>
> — @buddhaquotes__

If you had past or present experiences of poverty, hunger, or a lack of resources, you might internalize a deep belief that you will never have enough. Ironically, it is these thoughts that create a scarcity mindset and *lacking-consciousness*, perpetuating scarcity into the future.

This belief that "I do not have everything I need" can be an extremely difficult cycle to shake even when circumstances improve and you gain access to more resources. The *lacking-consciousness* remains until released and supplanted by a new belief of "I have everything I need."

For those growing up in impoverished homes, this lack was and became their reality. Their consciousness formed in a reality of lack, but I do believe and know in my heart a new mindset of abundance can be created. Humans have incredible resilience, and no matter what circumstances you're facing, shifting your consciousness can be a powerful first step toward transformation.

It is true that a scarcity mindset often comes from real experiences of lack and struggle. But if you keep living from that place, it will only hold you back. The moment you begin shifting into a *having-consciousness*, you will start opening the doors to abundance, peace, and new possibilities.

Your life is God-given, and when you came into this world, you naturally believed that everything you needed would be provided. But before long, you may have started absorbing the beliefs of those around you, messages like "You're not good enough," "We can't afford that," or "That's not possible." Little by little, those ideas trained your sensitive, moldable mind away from the truth of God's abundance.

At some point, you may see the story of scarcity that has been controlling you. In that moment, you can choose to reprogram your mind and beliefs from a *lacking-consciousness* to the abundance of a *having-consciousness.*

One of the ways you can do that is by learning to embrace the present.

Embracing the Present

> *What's meant for you will find you, what stays serves your growth, and what goes will always make space for better.*
>
> — @manifest.chronicals

I know a lot of people whose lives are controlled by fear.

In any situation, what they see first and foremost are the possible negative outcomes. They replay the worst-case scenario in their minds over and over, and that ends up paralyzing them. In cases like this, fear doesn't serve any purpose except to block exciting possibilities and stop positive change from happening. Does this sound like you?

Entering the present and making decisions from a place of trust and faith in future opportunities and abundance leads to better decision-making. When you're living in fear of a past situation or worrying about your future—neither of which is happening right now—you rob yourself of the opportunity to live in the present, which is your most significant source of power!

In your spiritual practices, you must become present because this is the true key to success. As Eckhart Tolle writes in *The Power of Now*,[1] "Ask yourself what 'problem' you have right now, not next year, tomorrow, or five minutes from now. What is wrong with this moment?"

It's a great question! When you really stop to ask yourself this question, you'll often find that, at this moment, nothing is going catastrophically wrong. Tolle clearly illustrated through that question how our thoughts and emotions can keep us trapped in the past and future—fearing what's to come, or being sad about what has or could have been.

It's when you start going round and round in your head about what could go wrong next week, next month, or even next year, or looking back to your past and everything that hasn't worked out that things start to go wrong. More often than not, we get preoccupied with future problems—problems that are not happening at this moment.

---

1. Eckhart Tolle, *The Power of Now: A Guide to Spiritual Enlightenment*. Hachette Australia, 2011.

Choosing to live in the present moment is a gift you can give yourself right now. It is in the now that your true power lies: your decision-making, faith, and intuitive abilities. It's a challenge to keep the mind from drifting off into the past or the future; it's even harder to stay there for even a few minutes at a time, let alone consistently. The key is to sense the moment that you are in and be aware enough to question fear by asking yourself: *Is there anything wrong at this very moment?* If not, give a quick thanks to God for the present moment, where nothing is actually wrong!

One of the most common examples of a thought that takes people out of the present is that of not having enough money for the foreseeable future. That is quite understandable. But looping thoughts about what you do not have and the worst that could happen because of the money you don't have won't bring in more abundance. What will help is bringing your attention fully to this moment and taking stock of, and being grateful for, what you do have, and asking "With that, what can I do right now?" When you act from that place of presence and trust in God, the right ideas, people, and opportunities will begin to enter your consciousness in a way you couldn't have imagined.

You might also find yourself heartbroken over the loss of a relationship, believing you'll never love again. When your mind is struggling with the pain of lost love, you tend to forget all the countless gifts you currently do have. You forget the amount of beauty, love, and joy that is surrounding you at this moment: friends who care, the air that you breathe, and the love of God, who has never left your side.

All these challenges deserve time, feeling, care, and attention, but the key is to bring care into the present moment, not spiral into sadness about the past or worry about the future.

At this moment, all is well; you are alive and breathing. That is all you need to arrive at the next moment, the future version of yourself. Each day is built on hundreds of NOW moments, unfolding one after another.

If you live more often in the present moment, you'll soon find that, day by day, you are actually creating a reality that mirrors your wildest dreams!

How to Become More Present: Practical Tips

> *Awe, you see, is what moves us forward.*
>
> — Joseph Campbell

There are many ways you can practice being more present in your day-to-day activities.

For example, when you step into the shower and pour shampoo onto your hand, take a moment to breathe in the scent deeply before lathering it into your hair. This simple act engages your sense of smell and anchors you in the present moment.

Stopping to smell the roses is exactly what living in the present moment is all about. Upon waking up, take thirty seconds to be in the now. Feel what it's like to be in your body, in your room, on your bed.

This is an incredibly difficult practice in a society that glorifies living five minutes, five hours, or even five days ahead of the now! Thus, living in the moment requires focus. You have to bring your attention straight into the now and try to keep it there.

Helpful Tips to Grow Your New *Having-Consciousness*

> *"Happiness is not about getting all you want, it's about enjoying all that you have."*
>
> — Unknown Author

What new actions can you take to shift into a *having-consciousness*, leaving your *scarcity-consciousness* behind? By taking small actions in your immediate environment, you remind yourself of the abundance of the world in and around you, and this will set you up for success.

Reinforce Abundance Through Simple Actions

If you can, keep the things you use and love nearby and in good condition. Maybe it's a favorite food, a journal, or a pair of shoes that makes you feel grounded. Treat these as reminders that you are cared for. I personally like to keep enough cash in my wallet and enough stock of food and vitamins in my pantry. This helps my consciousness stay in an abundant state, allowing my heart to know that I always have enough.

If resources are limited, you can still express a *having-consciousness* by keeping your space tidy, showing gratitude for what you have, or sharing kindness with someone else. Each act signals to your consciousness, *I have enough right now.*

Shift Gently When Feelings of Lack Arise

When you notice fear—about money, time, or loss—pause and remind yourself that the feeling is temporary. Focus on the present. In this moment, you have breath, awareness, and the ability to choose peace. That's the foundation of a *having-consciousness.*

By keeping your inner and outer world "well stocked" with gratitude, awareness, and trust, you create room for more to flow. I've found that when I focus less on what I don't have and more on what is already present, life keeps showing me how supported I truly am. It's a simple practice, but the changes it brings are profound and magical!

Pray from Abundance

> *In order to manifest you must assume the feeling of wish being fulfilled. You must be able to feel it in your body long before your senses are aware of it [...] you make the shift from believing to knowing, and what you absolutely know is not tinged with doubt.*
>
> — Wayne Dyer

Dr. Roger Teel of Centers for Spiritual Living said, "Most people pray amiss." He explained it like this: When you're in a drought and you pray for rain, you're actually praying from lack—you're affirming that rain isn't here. But if you take the word *for* out of your prayer and instead "pray rain" while visualizing pouring rain, something changes. You begin to see, feel, and know rain. You imagine the smell of wet earth, the sound of drops on your roof, the relief and joy of receiving and then having what you need. That is praying *from* abundance instead of *for* abundance.

This same principle applies to any prayer or desire you might have. When you focus on wanting, you create more of the energy of wanting. When you focus on having, you align with the results you are desiring!

Always remember: Wanting equals more wanting!

Keep Your Word

> *Before you speak, let your words pass through three gates: Is it true, is it necessary, is it kind?*
>
> — Unknown Author

Keeping your word is one of the most powerful ways to build a *having-consciousness*. When you follow through on what you say—whether that's showing up for a friend, paying a bill, finishing a task, or being on time—you strengthen the message to your consciousness that you can be trusted, that you are enough, and that you have enough.

Whether it's financial or otherwise, I try my best to do what I say I'm going to do. One of the personal agreements I've made with the Universe is to keep my word with everything I commit to—especially when it comes to money. For me, that means never borrowing without a clear plan for how I will repay it. But for you, that agreement might look different. You might be in a season where you need to borrow or ask for help—and that's okay. What matters most is your intention: to do what you can, when you can, with honesty and faith. If you make a promise and cannot fulfill it as planned, communicate with openness and integrity. That's still keeping your word—it shows the Universe that you are moving in a vibrational state of truth instead of fear.

When I was twenty-two, I needed $2,000 for the down payment on my first home. I borrowed the amount from my father, and I was determined not only to pay him back but to do it early—and I did. That experience taught me that when I honor my word, I tell the Universe, "I am enough, and I have enough."

Keeping your word, in whatever way you can, is an act of abundance. It shows your consciousness—and the Universe itself—that you are reliable, capable, and open to receiving more.

Don't Make Choices from Fear—You'll Always Be Taken Care Of

One evening in Colombia, I went out for a massage and dinner. I brought just enough cash to cover both, leaving my wallet at home. When I finished, I had about seven or eight dollars left.

Normally, I carry my wallet in my pocket, but that night, for some reason, I chose not to. Looking back, that simple choice turned out to be the Universe taking care of me.

As I was walking home, I suddenly felt something wet hit my shoulder—bird poop, I assumed. Almost instantly, a woman appeared beside me, all concerned, offering to help clean me up. While she kept my attention on the "mess," her partner quietly pickpocketed me.

When I got home, I realized what had happened. They'd taken the few dollars I had left. Normally, I would've had my wallet with me, filled with over a hundred dollars and all my credit cards. But not that night.

I could have reacted by becoming more guarded and suspicious, telling myself to never carry my wallet again. But that's how fear and lack sneak into your consciousness. Instead, I chose to see it differently. I learned to stay more aware of my surroundings, yes—but I also chose to keep carrying my wallet as an act of trust, as a declaration to the Universe that I am provided for.

When you develop your consciousness into one of love, happiness, and abundance, more doors open. When you don't allow paranoia into your consciousness, you will always be taken care of.

> *Learn to exchange fears, doubts, and uncertainties for faith. Faith can make you whole. Faith can convert fear into certainty, poverty in riches, disease into health. Faith can lift you from the valley of despair into a mountain of hope and certainty.*
>
> — Ernest Holmes

A Life-Changing Lesson

The first time I was introduced to a *having-consciousness* was when I was sixteen.

Like most teenagers, I didn't have much money. When I started driving my first car, I only put enough gas in the tank to reach the halfway mark. I told myself I was being sensible, stretching every dollar as far as I could. Eventually, that habit caught up with me. One afternoon, I ran out of gas.

My grandfather came to tow my car home, shaking his head the whole way. When we arrived, he gave me a piece of advice that would stay with me to this day. He said, "It's just as easy to keep the top half of your tank full as it is to keep the bottom half full."

At sixteen, I thought he was just telling me to stop making him come rescue me. But what he was really doing was planting the seed of abundance in my consciousness.

That simple metaphor reminded me that when you make decisions from the vibrational state of having, your reality shifts. You stop waiting until you're running on empty to fill yourself back up, whether that means your energy, your love, or your resources.

When you believe you already have what you need, you move with confidence, you trust more deeply, and you receive blessings without questioning it too much. You start to see the world as a generous place, as a playground of opportunity.

You start to live in God-consciousness, where opportunities flow toward you rather than away from you.

One practice above all others has the power to bring you into God-consciousness: meditation.

Chapter Four

The Benefits of Meditation

> “*When you spend your time in meditation, connecting with your source, don't ever ask or want for anything, be quiet and still in the silence, and life will just show up in grand and glorious ways.*
>
> —*Joel Goldsmith*

Meditation is one of the most direct ways to Seek the Kingdom and create the life you truly desire.

My regular meditation practice has kept my faith strong. It's the time of day I set aside to sit, clear my thoughts, and commune with God. During meditation, I get to take a break, let my thoughts dissipate, and just be. This time of silence will help you create your reality from within God-consciousness—a place of harmony, flow, and wisdom—instead of struggling to build from human-consciousness—a place of constant struggle where everything is about striving, control, and effort.

Meditation allows you to enjoy a smoother, more enjoyable life experience on the God-consciousness trail.

My goal is to help you find the smoothest path from human-consciousness to God-consciousness.

Meditation is the most powerful way to achieve this.

The Practice of Meditation

> *Success blooms in the garden of tranquility. Take a serene moment today to meditate and nurture your inner peace.*
>
> — Unknown Author

Body Postures and Meditation Styles

What is the best way to position the body when entering a meditative state? It depends on you and the needs of your body. Personally, I don't use the traditional posture seen in photos and at meditation retreats—sitting erect with legs crossed in the lotus position—because this posture creates unnecessary strain on my body.

My goal is to have no pressure or tension anywhere in my body. In fact, I don't want to feel my body at all while meditating. Therefore, I make adjustments to be completely comfortable and totally relaxed during meditation.

For fourteen years, I meditated in a round bamboo papasan chair at my home in Morrison, Colorado. When I moved to Colombia, I lived in a hotel for about two years and had to make do with what was available. For the first year, I meditated on my bed, which wasn't the best place for sinking as deeply into meditation as I preferred. Once I found a comfortable chair—a Lovesac shipped from the US—I was able to reach those meditative depths I'd been accustomed to in Colorado.

Finding the right chair or the most comfortable place to relax your body allows you to concentrate on deepening into the silence, rather than focusing on any discomfort.

There are many methods of meditation taught widely around the world, as well as many supportive environments for practice. Some involve sitting in silence, following a guided meditation, tuning into binaural beats (two tones creating a third tone), listening to calming music while sitting or lying down, or chanting mantras. The meditation style that has worked best for me is simply sitting in silence, focusing on my heart center, and clearing my mind. This approach has proven itself over and over to be profound and effective.

I've received advice from various teachers and gurus to meditate on an empty stomach, and I've certainly noticed that my meditations flow better when I do. If your blood is working to digest food and your body is focused on that process, achieving a deeper connection with God through meditation becomes more difficult.

Sample Meditation: Gratitude

Let's get started with a simple meditation practice I frequently use: mindful encouragement. Find a quiet place to sit in the most comfortable chair or position available to you. Allow your body to relax completely so you won't need to think about physical discomfort throughout your meditation. Close your eyes, take some time to give thanks, and begin clearing your thoughts, allowing yourself to rest in the silence.

Begin with the words, "Thank you, God, for this beautiful day!" Then continue silently verbalizing affirmations. As you say each one, visualize what it means to you personally. Following are some affirmations that I visualize, but I encourage you to create your own images that resonate with your heart:

"I am loving," giving and receiving love throughout my day. "I feel very loved." *I visualize myself hugging the most precious people in my world and feeling that warmth and connection.*

"I am happy," giving and receiving happiness throughout my day. "I feel very happy." *I see myself skipping, feeling joyful and free.*

"I am healthy." I scan my body and say, "I'm in optimum perfect health. I feel very healthy." *I visualize scanning my body—from my head, down to my chest, stomach, legs, and feet—affirming that I am very healthy.*

"I am wealthy," affirming I have enough money to live the rest of my life comfortably and to help people in need along the way. "I feel very wealthy." *I visualize stacks and stacks of money, pallets full of it. I see a line of people wait-*

ing, and I'm handing out the money to each person, one by one.

"I am wise," affirming my intelligence in all that I am. "I feel very wise." *I visualize myself doing things that represent wisdom to me: remembering names and numbers; writing, editing, and publishing a book; building multiple successful businesses; and learning Spanish. Some things I'm good at, some I'm still learning, but all are part of being wise.*

Then reaffirm: "I am loving, I am happy, I am healthy, I am wealthy, I am wise!"

And, "I feel loved, I feel happy, I feel healthy, I feel wealthy, I feel wise!"

Through this process, I begin shedding the outside world and moving into a deeper, more profound connection with God. I encourage you to try your own version of this meditation. After the visualizations, simply sit and follow your breath for the remainder of the time you have allotted. This part can be tricky, especially when beginning a new meditation practice. The key is to quiet the mind as best you can.

Following are a couple of strategies that have helped me improve my meditation practice. Hopefully, you'll be able to use some of my methods to create a unique practice that works best for you.

Keep It Simple

> *Meditation means you just shut up. If you just shut up, everything that needs to happen to you will happen to you.*
>
> — Sadhguru

I personally don't use complex meditation techniques or any special mantras. You really don't need to say or do anything special to connect with God. You just need to sit down, close your eyes, and relax into the silence. It's as simple as that. The act of communing with God will take care of the rest.

When I began my practice, I would sit in a wooden chair, work on clearing my mind, and relax into the silence. (As I progressed, I found that a cushioned chair supports deeper meditation.)

As early as grammar school, I didn't enjoy reading and couldn't understand why. Later, as an adult, I was diagnosed with a learning disability. So you can rest assured that learning to meditate doesn't require a degree—all you need is the right intention, and that alone will propel you on to your journey.

Take the time to sit in meditation, if possible, more than once a day, and say to God, "I'm here." If you dedicate yourself to your meditation practice, God will help you with the rest.

Center Your Focus to Quiet the Mind

When thoughts jump in (and believe me, they will), lovingly and gently push them away and return to your center.

To get the most desirable results from your meditation practice, choose a focal point—a specific area of your body on which to direct your attention and energy. My sternum/heart center has worked magically for me, but if another area feels better for you, use that.

Each time my mind wanders and leaves the silence, I use a simple process to regain my center: I gently push the thoughts away, then move my focus to the back of my head, down my spine, and into my heart center.

If you're still struggling to quiet your mind, try shifting your attention to your breath—simply following each inhale and exhale can help anchor you back to your focal point. Please know that you will engage in this process many times as you meditate.

Once you've been meditating for a while, you will learn to remain in silence for extended periods without as much mental chatter. However, try not to get frustrated! It still happens to me even after decades of practice.

Remember to give thanks each time you feel like you've reached a new depth in your practice.

Meditation and Connection

I once read in a book on meditation that people want to know how they can tell if they've actually connected with God. The author shared that they would feel warmth all over their body. That's the divine place I desire to be, and I quite often find myself there. I can remember feeling the warm Colorado afternoon sun externally at the same time the warmth ran through my body from true communion with God internally, and I got lost in my meditations for one to two hours. I didn't want to come out.

At times, when I return from a deep meditation, my body is so fatigued that I can barely stand up for a little while afterward. This is perfectly normal when you've been in a deep meditative state. It can feel as though your body's energy is drained, and it actually is! You've just been deep in communion with God. I love that feeling because I know I've had a profound connection with Him.

People all over the world use a variety of methods to connect with God. As you get started in your meditation practice, you might find that recordings, music, or guided meditations help you enter a meditative state. For me personally, I found that only complete silence can facilitate a deep communion with God.

Be still, and know that I am God.

— Psalm 46:10

The Goal of Meditation

The true goal of meditation is to Seek the Kingdom and commune with God, not to fulfill your dreams or desires.

Many people approach meditation as a way of gaining or manifesting something, but meditation is not about asking God for favors or presenting Him with a wish list. Your wish list is your ego talking—and in my vocabulary, ego means Edging God Out.

If you truly Seek the Kingdom through your meditations, blessings will show up for you in grand and glorious ways. But if you go into meditation trying to get something, your list won't be fulfilled. This is the elegant contradiction that occurs as your awareness moves toward God-consciousness.

Matthew 6:33 captures the essence of Seeking the Kingdom and communing with your Creator perfectly: "But seek first his kingdom and his righteousness, and all these things will be given to you as well."

My suggestion is to enter the practice of meditation

with the sole intention of connecting with your Source. If you can truly seek God only for communion, you won't have to want or desire anything ever again.

Seek God in any form you can: Spend time in meditation, read spiritual books, seek out a guru, or attend uplifting self-development seminars. If you seek God alone and do not ask for anything, you will remain open to miracles.

Meditation allows you to Seek the Kingdom, calm the outside world in the silence, and commune with the Creator, opening the door to God's divine gifts.

Wanting and Desiring

So why is it that by not asking for anything, you begin to receive?

When you want something, this feeling of wanting removes you from the state of receiving. Wanting pushes you to ask for things in your meditation, which makes it more challenging to remain receptive. In wanting, you become attached to a particular outcome and set up expectations. You may start to view God as a wish-giver, and this expectation closes your eyes to the ways life is truly available to you. The Universe always knows what's best for you.

Walking around in a space of "wanting-ness" creates a lack within your consciousness. You don't want to train your consciousness to notice only what's missing. If you focus on abundance and what you already have—giving thanks for all of it—the energy of the Universe will give you more and more of what you desire.

Seeking the Kingdom doesn't mean wanting things, for things exist uniquely in human-consciousness. Engaging in wanting results in the cultivation of a taker's mentality, where nothing you get ever feels like it's enough. This is going to set you up for constant disappointment.

When you Seek the Kingdom, you transcend into God-consciousness, where the things you want and desire already exist, and all that you need to do is be receptive to all the blessings that are coming your way.

If communion is truly your only desire, then *all things shall be added unto you*.

My success started early when I learned to Seek the Kingdom for no reason other than to commune with God and be open to His miracles every day. I wasn't following a method, mantra, or affirmation. I was just there in those moments with myself and God. Yet my journey continued to get better and more miraculous as I continued to Seek the Kingdom.

Chasing What We Want

Constantly chasing after what you want is like chasing butterflies. The more you run after them, the faster they fly away from you.

Relationships provide an extraordinary example: Many of us have chased love, but more often than not, chasing love doesn't actually work.

What will draw blessings toward you is the act of working on your energy—shifting and changing your consciousness to become the best version of yourself you can be. When you are moving and making decisions from positive vibrational states (joy, health, love, happiness, etc.), what you want out of life will begin to come to you more easily. On the other hand, when you are functioning from a negative vibrational state (fear, paranoia, stress, anger, etc.), you will begin chasing and will never be in the state of openness that is required to receive.

Nature provides a magnificent example of how we can exist in energetic alignment. Simply witnessing how nature blooms and grows—no flower or tree comparing itself to another—reminds me of what's possible in our lives. All of nature is blossoming and merely being, each flower and tree molding to its ecosystem according to its needs without asking for or desiring anything different. Nature is a manifestation of God-given beauty. It is an example of what is possible if you stop grasping for things you think you want and learn to simply allow yourself to be your magnificent self! Treat yourself as if you were nature, and be the magnificent flower or tree you're meant to be.

You might think that chasing some job, object, or relationship will improve how you feel, but it has been proven to me time and time again that we humans don't actually know what's best for us. Only God does. None of us can ever outthink, outgive, or outplan God.

If you sit in the silence of meditation, a deep connection between you and God will be born, and your experiences will be more grand and glorious without ever having to ask Him for anything.

What Does Seeking the Kingdom Look Like?

> *The kingdom of God is not in a time or in any place. It is like lightning—it is here, there and everywhere. And it has no time and place because the kingdom of God that I preach is within YOU.*
>
> — Inspired by Luke 17:20-21

Seeking the Kingdom isn't limited to meditation alone—it's a way of being. Here are some of the ways I've Sought the Kingdom over the past forty years. Please see how they feel to you.

Reading Spiritual Books

In my twenties and thirties, I read books on spirituality, meditation, consciousness, and personal growth—and what a treasure trove of wisdom I discovered! Books like Anita Moorjani's *Dying to Be Me*, Eckhart Tolle's *The Power of Now*, and Joel Goldsmith's incredible works *Practicing the Presence, Realization of Oneness, The Infinite Way*, and *Living Between Two Worlds*, opened my mind to new possibilities and reinforced the message I was hearing from multiple sources: Meditation and seeking God were the keys to happiness, health, and success.

Attending Seminars and Retreats

I attended countless self-development seminars and retreats during those formative years. Being in a room with like-minded seekers and learning from experienced teachers accelerated my growth in ways I couldn't have achieved alone.

Seeking Out Teachers, Mentors, and Gurus

My spiritual mentors taught me the importance of communing with God and what made it so powerful. I've been blessed to find incredible teachers. Jim Lewis at the Unity Church of Denver was an early guide. Then I met Dr. Roger Teel—the man who would end up being my minister and teacher for over thirty years—at the Centers for Spiritual Living in Lakewood, Colorado. I met my most impactful mentor, Reverend Al Heard, at a retreat in Wyoming. And I connected with Sadhguru's wisdom through Instagram. Mentors can appear anywhere—spiritual centers, retreats, online platforms—so stay open and actively seek them out!

I knew I needed to put the Kingdom first, despite it not always being easy to find time while working, raising children, and managing the demands of day-to-day living. Yet once I made up my mind, there was no going back. I stayed committed to meditation and all the other spiritual practices I'd cultivated, and that commitment has shaped everything that followed.

When We Stop Seeking the Kingdom

Since beginning my meditation practice, numerous gifts have simply shown up; dream cars, fancy homes, condos, and a privileged, luxurious lifestyle became available for me to access.

Somewhere along the way, I made an unconscious choice and stopped seeking God.

I stopped meditating, attending seminars, and Seeking the Kingdom. I got busy enjoying all these alluring material gifts I had received, and my seeking went on the back burner. I began attributing my success to my ego and allowing a lifestyle driven by wealth and possessions to take over.

What Happened?

Due to my newfound confidence in my egoic mind, I began to experience exactly what my reality would look like without my daily meditations and spiritual journeying. I watched it all plummet to rock bottom.

I stopped meditating, reading, learning, and investing in my spiritual journey for about six-to-twelve months.

Crazily enough, my ego enabled this to happen not only once, but twice in my life.

The first time was in Utah, which I mentioned earlier. The second time happened in 1988. I had been managing and co-owning Sunset Beach Fitness and Racket Club since 1986, and once again, I was living the dream. I had a great income, comfortable lifestyle, all the material success I could want. In just two years, I let my ego overtake my connection with God once again.

Out of nowhere, the majority owner handed me back my $10,000 investment and said, "We're done." He let me go on the spot. I had a house I needed to liquidate quickly, and suddenly everything I had built was gone.

Both times that I began overidentifying with my ego and human-consciousness, I ended up crushed and bankrupt.

If it had only happened once, one could say my finances collapsing was a fluke or coincidence, but to me the connection with Seeking the Kingdom feels intuitively undeniable. Two different times, everything crashed to the bottom, and I lost 100 percent of everything. But after the second time, I promised myself I would never stop Seeking the Kingdom again, and I'm here to say that since I initiated my spiritual practices again in 1988, I've remained steadfast and consistent in my pursuit of the Kingdom, and things have been soaring to greater and greater heights. *Amen*!

This proved to me that when I'm not seeking God through my daily meditations or all the enriching spiritual books and seminars, things take a downward turn because I slip back into living in human-consciousness.

Why Did I Stop Meditating?

I don't feel as though it was a conscious decision; rather, I allowed my enjoyment of this intoxicating new reality to take my focus. Just like when I get caught up in a passing thought in meditation, I became caught up and identified with all the luxury I was experiencing. In doing so, I let my EGO begin to take over. I thought I no longer needed to 'Seek' the Kingdom since I felt I had 'arrived' due to everything I was now enjoying.

The ego has a funny way of using our spirituality to try and trap us, attempting to bring us back into human-consciousness. The ego says, "I am spiritual, so I don't need to seek God anymore." This often happens after great spiritual experiences and material success; the ego uses these experiences as bait to get us to identify with human-consciousness once again.

I felt like I had found the Holy Grail, so I no longer needed to search.

This couldn't have been farther from the truth. All our actions must always stay in alignment with Seeking the Kingdom if we are to remain on the path. It is the act of searching and turning inward that must guide our every step. Many of us turn to God during hard moments and give up when things get back on track. I am here to tell you that you must Seek the Kingdom when times are difficult, and continue to give thanks and remain in a state of Seeking the Kingdom even when all is well.

How Did I Rebuild My Life for Even Greater Success?

After seeing it so profoundly twice, I absolutely knew that trying to live in human-consciousness alone wasn't working for me. I got quiet once again in my renewed daily meditation and started reading spiritual books and attending spiritual seminars. This is something any of us can do starting today; we simply have to make a conscious effort to do so.

It took seven years to rebuild, and those years were focused on spiritual growth and learning.

When you encounter a wall, the Universe forces you to take a turn. My turn led me to manage the Boys and Girls Club of Metro Denver, which led me to run their car donation program. I learned the business inside and out for two years, discovering along the way that my true calling was in helping charities. God truly puts you in places so you can succeed down the road!

Eventually, I reached out to Big Brothers Big Sisters of America, pitching to help them set up their own car donation program. That's when my income tripled, and by 1995, I could safely say things were heading uphill again.

I decided to listen to all my teachers and mentors, and

prioritized Seeking the Kingdom. I eventually started my own car donation business—Cars Helping Charities—in 2002, continued growing it for twelve years, and eventually sold it. I invested the profits from the sale of my business (along with my life savings) into a wealth management company, and my investment ended up growing fivefold over the next ten years.

I now live in Colombia, where my days are more abundant and magical than I ever could have imagined!

Finding the Time

At my busiest, I found creative ways to carve out an extra hour every day. Picture this: I was a single dad raising two children on my own. I would wake up at 5 a.m. before the kids were up to meditate for an hour.

Deep in my heart, I knew that if I wished for my reality to keep expanding, I needed to find more time to Seek the Kingdom. An idea came to me.

During this period, I was the car donation manager for the Boys and Girls Club, working alone in a warehouse. One day, I found an old wicker seat cover in a donated car. I took it into the warehouse bathroom, put it on the toilet seat, and meditated there during my workday. I knew no one would bother me since I was often the only person in the building. This gave me the extra hour of meditation I was desperately seeking.

Joel Goldsmith teaches in his writings that if you meditate a minimum of four times daily, your identity can consistently rest in God-consciousness. I interpret this to mean that if you create a couple of opportunities to meditate for thirty minutes to an hour throughout the day, plus one or two shorter spurts of ten-to-twenty minutes, you can begin residing more and more within God-consciousness.

The longer periods of meditation provide an opportunity to go deeper within. I've noticed in my own practice that it can take nearly twenty minutes just to shed the outside world. I meditate twice a day, for around forty-five minutes to two hours per session. This has been helpful in my journey.

But not all meditations must be long and deep, especially when you are first starting out. Even ten or fifteen minutes is a great foundational step. Eventually, as you get deeper into your practice, it will become easier and more comfortable to sit for longer periods—and in fact, it might become a space you don't want to leave.

Consistency Is Key

Regardless of whether you are a novice or expert, consistency is essential for a healthy meditation practice.

Dr. Teel, a mentor of mine, likens the practice of meditation to that of a car battery. He explains that if you don't start your car on a regular basis, your battery will drain, meaning you won't be able to start your car when you need it. For this reason, meditating on a regular basis is essential.

If you're not routinely meditating and caring for your energy, the gears and pistons of your life won't turn and fire the way you need them to. If you practice meditation consistently and often, your internal battery remains charged so that when you need to use it, it's there, rumbling and ready to power the miraculous reality you're creating.

For the majority of my years' worth of meditation, I've been able to maintain a practice of sitting at least two times a day. I build my day around my meditation schedule instead of letting the day dictate when I choose to meditate. I meditate for at least forty-five minutes when I first wake up, and again in the middle of the afternoon for another forty-five minutes or more, sneaking in smaller meditations of about ten-to-fifteen minutes wherever possible—just enough to always keep my spirit focused on communing and connecting with God.

No Excuses!

One thing that has stuck with me throughout the years is the advice Reverend Heard gave to his congregants.

People would often tell Reverend Heard, "I simply

can't afford the time it takes to meditate." The Reverend would always answer, "But you can't afford *not* to." Now, after meditating for decades and watching blessings multiply as a result, I wholeheartedly agree.

Here's the paradox: The more time I give to meditation, the more time I seem to have. Everything flows more smoothly, decisions become clearer, and opportunities appear effortlessly. It absolutely works.

Several years ago, Dr. Teel, then the senior minister at Mile Hi Church in Colorado, invited me to share my story at a Sunday service. He'd heard about the remarkable life I was living despite having hit rock bottom a couple of times, and he wanted his congregation to hear it.

I accepted the invitation because I wanted to share a simple truth: I'm not special or different. What worked for me can work for anyone. No matter what your circumstances are—whether you're rich or poor, thriving or struggling—you can meditate.

This is the way of God. He's given us a way to connect and commune no matter our circumstances. You don't need money, special equipment, or a perfect environment. You can connect anywhere, at any time. So please don't come up with excuses, because you can't afford not to meditate if you want a magical existence filled with everything you desire.

As you deepen your meditation practice and learn to Seek the Kingdom consistently, something remarkable will begin to unfold. You'll start to notice that what happens to you isn't random. There's a divine intelligence guiding you, opening doors, and orchestrating events in ways you could never have planned yourself. This is what I call the Divine Plan, and understanding how it works will transform the way you see everything.

Chapter Five

The Divine Plan

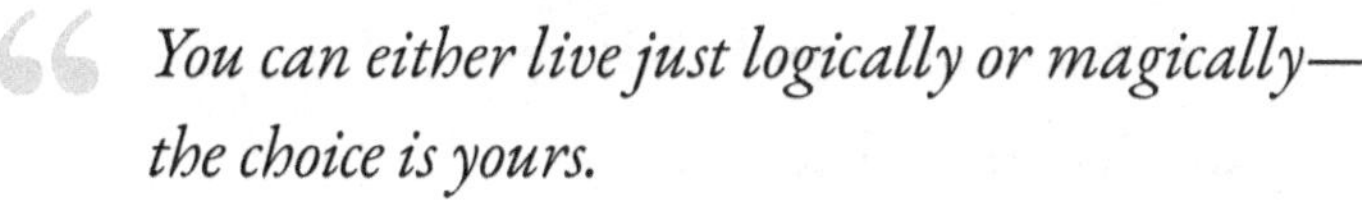

> *You can either live just logically or magically—the choice is yours.*
>
> — Sadhguru

We can predict our future by creating it.

Let's define what goes into a Divine Plan. What is predestined and what is left up to free will?

Predestiny

Predestiny (or predestination) is the captivating belief that our lives are like an intricately scripted play, written in concert between our souls and God—or a higher power or cosmic force, if you will—before we're born.

I believe our souls work in partnership with God to craft our experiences in every lifetime to provide our souls with optimal conditions for growth. Perhaps only the significant milestones are predestined: the date we're born (which gives us our astrological identity), the family we're born into, the major relationships we'll have, the children we may birth, the career path we'll follow, and the key challenges we'll face.

In my view, predestination does not dictate every detail and circumstance of our lives. This is where we have the opportunity to exercise our free will and choice. However, it seems likely that the general outline of our lives is established in a soul contract—an agreement we make with God that determines the details of our new incarnation. (We'll go into soul contracts in more depth in the next chapter.)

Imagine a cosmic plan orchestrated by God that works with and through us. In this scenario, the plotline of our lives has already been carefully crafted. Before we take our first breath, our roles, major experiences, and challenges are partially scripted—as if we are characters in a remarkable story with room to improvise.

This concept invites us to ponder profound questions: If our major milestones are largely predetermined, then what is within our power to shape, change, and choose? How does our consciousness play a role in predestiny? Does our sense of personal responsibility hold any meaning in this cosmic play?

These philosophical questions have ignited intense debates throughout history, and they're worth contemplating as we explore what it means to live in alignment with the Divine Plan.

Free Will

> *The man who has no inner life is the slave of his surroundings.*
>
> — Henri Frédéric Amiel

Free will refers to our agency, our ability to self-determine, our ability to choose.

While I believe that certain milestones in our lives are predestined, I also believe that God has given us the gift of free will—the freedom to make choices every day. Between the major events that shape your life, you are constantly making choices: what you eat, what you think, what you say, and how you respond to others.

Every one of these choices matters, because whatever you think, feel, say, and do becomes who you are. Life doesn't just happen to you, it happens through you! Your consciousness is the domain of your free will. Through the exercise of this free will, you become an active participant in the Divine Plan. You may not be able to rewrite the predestined milestones of your story, but you can choose the tone, the pace, and the energy with which you live them.

These are the conscious decisions that shape not only your experiences in this lifetime, but the evolution of your soul across many lifetimes to come.

The Contradiction

Let's untangle the contradiction between predestination and free will. When you choose to live in human-consciousness, it's difficult to see the miracles and divine assistance available to you. Yet when you choose to create from within God-consciousness, you experience predestination as a force to partner with, conspire with, and cocreate alongside—allowing you to fully realize all the miracles and abundance available along the way to your predestined milestones.

I believe that if something is meant to happen, it will —predestination takes precedence. Major events are preordained based on the work we've done with our consciousness in our current and past lifetimes. However, we still have the free will to choose how we reach those outcomes. This influences how our souls learn and evolve in this lifetime.

My friend Claudia's experience clearly illustrates this

idea. She has immense faith and a daily meditation practice, and she chooses to live in God-consciousness. When trying to decide whether to get a place in Armenia or Medellín, she diligently researched both options. Despite her preference for Medellín, she couldn't find anything suitable there.

Ultimately, Claudia kept her heart open to all possibilities rather than limiting her search. Before long, her mother reached out with news that she had found the perfect apartment in Armenia—only half a mile from where Claudia's parents and pregnant sister lived. It was exactly what she'd been looking for. Having Claudia near her family seemed to be the predestined will of the Universe.

To me, the move was preordained and already laid out through her consciousness—planned in the divine mind, with the timing just needing to line up. By being open, having faith, and relying on God-consciousness, she knew she'd find the right option. She maintained her peace and allowed God to guide her, trusting herself to cocreate with what was already predestined.

I believe there is a grand pattern to our lives, and that we will ultimately arrive exactly where we are meant to be. Our destination is our destiny, predetermined as part of a larger design.

You always have a choice in how you reach your destination, much like traveling to a new city. If you want to travel from Denver, Colorado to Sedona, Arizona, you could drive, fly, or take a train or bus. If you drive, you'll have various roads and highways to choose from. While the routes differ, the end goal remains the same—you'll arrive in Sedona.

Your spiritual destination is already laid out, and the plan is unfolding with or without your conscious participation. By meditating and focusing on Seeking the Kingdom, you flow toward your destiny more smoothly, without as many roadblocks, bumps, and detours along the way.

Metaphorically, God has given you a room—your personal universe. The space is a gift, but how you furnish it is up to you. You pick the paint color, the houseplants on the windowsill, the art on the walls, the way the furniture sits. That's free will; the room is yours to shape.

So how will you furnish yours: with the clutter and chaos of human-consciousness or the spacious calm of God-consciousness?

Lessons from My Divine Plan

Our journey is ultimately about our soul's growth and expansion, as well as the joy of simply being alive and having fun. Everything has been exactly what it was supposed to be, creating the lessons and growth I needed this time around.

I believe we choose our parents through soul contracts, along with our childhood experiences and ultimate destiny. Growing up, I didn't get a whole lot of physical love from my parents and extended family. I wasn't raised in a touchy-feely family prone to hugging and physical affection—it was more of a whoop-your-ass-with-a-belt kind of family that always kept us in line. Love came in the form of a house to live in, food on the table at dinner time, and presents on the holidays.

My childhood wasn't a fairy tale, but I have come to see how it set me on the exact path I needed to arrive where I am today. If my parents had been more affectionate, I wouldn't have learned the lessons I needed for my highest growth. I created soul contracts with my parents for a reason, and that was part of the Divine Plan from the beginning.

What my parents *did* give me was far more valuable in the long run: They introduced me to metaphysical concepts and provided a spiritual foundation that has supported me during both the toughest and most joyful times in my life.

I was born into a spiritual family and community. During my early and adolescent years, we attended Unity Church of Denver. At eighteen, I realized I needed to explore my spirituality more deeply, so I began studying with Reverend Jim Lewis, a well-read and knowledgeable minister. By twenty-one, I sought further guidance from mentors and teachers at what was then the Religious Science Church.

As I mentioned in the first chapter, this foundation gave me something to return to during times of turmoil. Even during the moments when I forgot to focus on my spirituality and got caught up in outward, material pursuits—which always led to things falling apart—I had the tools to find my way back. This spiritual foundation my parents gave me has been my lifeline, and I owe them a great deal of gratitude for initiating me on this journey.

Everything you think, feel, say, and do becomes you—because nothing happens to you that doesn't happen through you. This is why you have to surrender and let go of anything that's not serving you or moving you forward.

Surrendering/Letting Go

I've come to recognize a trend. When something doesn't feel right, I worry endlessly about it, asking myself or God, "Why is this happening? Why is this in my life?"

At some point during each difficult situation, after enough worrying, I would arrive at a realization: "For some reason, this situation is part of my experience." While it was tempting to blame these challenges on God, I eventually understood that whatever happens to you happens through you, and these situations were ultimately for my highest good. I was creating these experiences to learn from them and to deepen my reliance on my faith in God. Each challenge highlighted areas where I still lacked faith. Finally, I discovered how beneficial it was to lean into the discomfort rather than push back against it.

Often I want to fix the difficulty and tension that I'm experiencing, but my mind can't fix them!

What truly helps me during challenging times is realizing that I need to surrender to whatever lesson God wants me to learn. I accept the situation by saying, "Okay, it's here. I don't know why this is happening, and it doesn't feel good, but I will stop trying to figure it out and let go. I choose to surrender to it and find peace."

When an obstacle appears, our human mind may look at it as a negative, saying, "It's wrong and it should be different," which creates fear and anxiety. As fast as we can surrender to the difficulty is how fast we will overcome it. Knowing there's a plan, that God is speaking to us and trying to guide us in a new direction for our highest good, can give us the strength needed to surrender to what is present—however painful.

If you're walking down a path and encounter a wall, you'll need to veer right or left. You may even have to leave the comfortable path you're on altogether. Yes, you may find yourself on a path of uncertainty, but please try to embrace it! Get your limited human perspective out of the way and allow the grandeur of God-consciousness to enrich you.

If something isn't flowing smoothly, it's likely not aligned with your highest good. When things are meant to be, the right path will emerge before you and guide you gently along. I've learned there's a perfect rhythm to everything. When you flow with it, magic unfolds.

The more you ruminate, the more you develop depression, anxiety, and fear, and risk remaining stuck in that mindset. This makes it harder to follow the path God has intended for you. Conversely, if you choose to let go and instead focus on relaxing and cultivating faith, you can navigate challenges more smoothly.

I am by no means beyond this. When something is giving me anxiety or fear, I still have to remind myself, "Stop being attached to the outcome and let it go." It is at this point that the path God has laid out for me begins to become visible again. When I let it go and choose to stop feeling fear—totally, 100 percent let go—the answers from God show up, and the problem magically fixes itself.

Now when negative feelings arise, I remind myself: I've been down this path before, and worrying doesn't help. There's a reason all of this is happening, and I need to relax into it and be at peace.

When the Universe wants you to be somewhere and wants you to do something, be patient. The pathways will eventually open easily and effortlessly for your safe arrival. Your only job is to surrender!

> *"When you begin to understand this life principle, you will know that there is a wellspring of life, substance, and intelligence within you, and that yours is the privilege at any time of giving way to its flow.*
>
> — *Eric Butterworth*

Learning to Listen

In 1988, I was let go from my position at a health club. The club returned a $10,000 investment I had made, and with this cash available, I began looking for investment opportunities. A member of the health club shared that he had quadrupled his father's money in the financial markets.

I was intrigued and agreed to open a brokerage account with him. Firm after firm turned me down, stating that I didn't have sufficient net worth. This turned out to be the Universe talking to me but I wasn't listening. We pushed on together, seeking out a firm that would take my $10,000. We eventually found one. I gave the gentleman my money to start making trades.

Within two weeks, I lost all of it.

Knowing what I know now, I can see that the Universe was providing me with roadblocks every time I was turned down—not to punish me but to advise and guide me. This story has helped me develop a deeper faith in surrendering to the Universe and the signs it provides.

After much practice, I've learned that when I encounter obstacles, it's best to surrender and turn toward the direction that God and my soul have designed for me.

Anita Moorjani's Story

The story of Anita Moorjani elegantly illustrates the vast power of letting go. In her book *Dying to Be Me*, she describes how she was dying of cancer and doing everything she could to heal herself for over four years:

I worked on forgiveness therapy and forgave everyone I knew—then forgave them again. I traveled through India and China, meeting Buddhist monks, Indian yogis, and enlightened masters, hoping that they'd help me find answers that would lead to my healing. I tried being vegan, meditating on mountaintops, yoga, ayurveda, chakra balancing, Chinese herbal medicine, pranic healing, and Chi Gong. But despite all this, my cancer just kept getting worse.[1]

After trying every possible treatment, her cancer remained. Weighing a mere seventy pounds, immobilized and exhausted, she finally gave up. She said, "Okay, God,

1. Anita Moorjani, *Dying to Be Me: My Journey from Cancer, to Near Death, to True Healing*, Carlsbad (Hay House LLC, 2015).

I'm done. I'm physically unable to do any more." In that moment, she finally let go. As she did, she returned from her near-death experience and was healed. Letting go was what she needed most of all.

After a four-year journey battling cancer, the only thing that brought her healing was surrendering to God. By letting go of her desire to fix and heal herself, she ultimately found true healing.

Understanding the Divine Plan—predestiny, free will, and surrender—has transformed how I experience life. I've learned that while the major milestones of my journey are already laid out, I have the power to choose whether I walk that path with ease or with struggle. By choosing to live in God-consciousness, Seeking the Kingdom through meditation, and surrendering to what is, I've discovered that experiences flow with a grace and magic I could never have orchestrated on my own.

However, the Divine Plan isn't just about this lifetime; it's part of a much larger journey—one that spans multiple lifetimes and provides our souls with countless opportunities to learn, grow, and evolve. Each life we live, each challenge we face, and each lesson we master contributes to our soul's eternal expansion. To truly understand the

Divine Plan, we must explore the cycle that makes it all possible: reincarnation.

Chapter Six

The Reincarnation Cycle

> *"Life and death, they're equal to this cosmos. We enter the material world and we go away again, reincarnated into something better."*
>
> — R. F. Kuang

What Is Reincarnation?

Reincarnation is a philosophical and spiritual paradigm that suggests individual souls and consciousness can be reborn into a new physical body after death. It is rooted in the idea that life is an ongoing cycle of birth, death, and rebirth, allowing the soul to experience multiple lifetimes in different forms and circumstances, and providing opportunities for growth in each journey.

Metaphorically, your body is a car, and your soul/consciousness is the driver. Through the passage of time, you may need to get a new car, but you remain the same driver. Death is simply a passage where the old model is traded in for a new one, lifetime after lifetime. What carries over is your consciousness and soul, starting right where you left off in your last life. That's why consciousness is ever evolving—you become more magnificent with each incarnation.

Every decade in sports, a figure emerges that expands the collective imagination of humanity—Roger Bannister breaking the four-minute mile and Michael Jordan's extraordinary natural ability comes to mind. Child prodigies like Mozart in music, Pascal in mathematics, and Picasso in painting display mind-bending talent at impossibly young ages.

I believe that skills and attributes developed in a past life are retained in our consciousness for our next birth. This remarkable phenomenon reflects consciousness evolving and expanding through the power of our desires, allowing our soul to grow even as our bodies are born, decay, and are reborn.

The opposite seems true to me as well. We carry over our burdens and unlearned lessons into our next incarnation. In my travels around the world, I've witnessed many forms of hardship, including deep poverty. These experiences remind me how mysterious the soul's journey really is. I don't pretend to know why some souls face greater challenges than others, but I believe that every lifetime offers its own opportunities for growth and awakening. For some, that growth might unfold through material struggle. For others, it might unfold through lessons of love, faith, resilience, or compassion. Only God truly knows the purpose behind each experience. What I've come to see is that no matter where we begin, our evolution depends on our willingness to grow and to become more aware, more faithful, and more loving than we were yesterday.

So many of our souls' lessons involve overcoming challenges and gaining the wisdom therein. I take it that if we face and thrive through these challenges, allowing ourselves to be guided into and by God-consciousness rather than staying stuck in the limited paradigm of human-consciousness, we may never have to face these challenges again in another lifetime.

It follows that in whatever state we leave our life, our consciousness and soul pick up right where we left off in the next iteration. If we continue working in this life toward living with expanded awareness, challenging ourselves to be the best version of ourselves as humanly possible, doing our absolute best to face all that comes toward us with an open heart, using every situation as a vehicle to access God-consciousness, developing faith, and surrendering more deeply to our intuition—these integrated lessons carry over into our next life.

What of those who choose to take their own lives?

When someone leaves this life through suicide, I hold only compassion for their pain and the impossible weight they carried. I believe the soul continues its journey, and there is a possibility that any unresolved lessons may resurface in future lifetimes—not as punishment but as another opportunity for healing. Yet this perspective should never be used to judge those who are suffering or those who have lost loved ones. In God-consciousness, we are all one. One person's struggle is all of our struggles. Personally, I try to do everything in my power to relieve another person's suffering when I can, because they are me and I am them.

Soul Contracts

In the realm of metaphysics and spirituality, the concept of soul contracts has attracted significant attention and intrigue. Soul contracts are believed to be pre-arranged agreements made between souls before they incarnate into physical bodies on Earth or possibly another planet in the galaxy.

These contracts involve encounters with other souls, specifying events and circumstances that provide us with opportunities for personal development, healing, and spiritual transformation. They are often profound and purposeful, shaping and influencing our earthly experiences, relationships, and personal growth. While soul contracts are subjective and spiritual in nature, they offer a unique perspective on the interconnectedness of individuals and the purpose behind our life's encounters and experiences with other souls on a similar journey.

Soul contracts are not strictly limited to romantic relationships, though these types of contracts can prove to be powerful catalysts for evolution. Your family of origin also represents soul contracts—your parents, siblings, and children are all souls you agreed to connect with before birth. Soul contracts can be made between any two souls before incarnating.

Why Are Soul Contracts Important?

Living Our Most Authentic Life

Soul contracts, as with other facets of the spiritual realm, are agreed upon for personal and consciousness development, healing, and spiritual transformation. I believe we create our soul contracts to propel us forward when we get comfortable or stuck, encouraging evolution over stasis.

Soul contracts help you use your experiences to remember your true nature as a divine soul connected to God. Whether through challenges or new opportunities, they push you to live more authentically and to the fullest extent possible here on Earth while maintaining a connection and awareness of your divine nature.

Lessons and Growth

Beyond living authentically, soul contracts are specifically designed to teach you critical lessons through direct experience. These lessons can span diverse themes like forgiveness, compassion, self-love, abundance, connection, overcoming addictions, and raising your consciousness to new levels. Each contract targets particular areas where your soul needs development, presenting you with the exact challenges and opportunities required for that growth.

Completion and Release

Soul contracts may have a specific time duration, serving a specific purpose. Once the intended lessons or growth opportunities are achieved, the contract may be fulfilled, and the souls may move on to new agreements or experiences.

This can explain why some souls leave the planet "early," at least what seems early from a human perspective.

Karmic Implications

Soul contracts are closely related to karma, which is a natural spiritual law of the Universe. In some soul contracts, you have the opportunity to fulfill karmic debts or obligations, rebalance energies, correct wrongs, and resolve past experiences from this lifetime or previous ones. Ultimately, these contracts represent the Universe's way of rebalancing itself.

The people you may have unconsciously hurt, or those who have hurt you, are often manifestations of karmic soul contracts established before your birth. Another way to understand this is through the lessons learned or left unlearned in past lives. If a lesson wasn't fully embraced, soul contracts may be created in your next lifetime to ensure that lesson is completed.

It doesn't make sense to think that God or the Universe randomly assigns people good or bad lives; God is pure love, enveloping us in love and nothing else. Therefore, all painful experiences and relationships can be viewed as contracts that enable your growth. At any moment, you can choose to change your perspective and understand why these experiences happened.

When you finally move through inevitable painful experiences here on Earth—after resisting it, grieving it, and accepting it for what it was—you are often left with a loving connection once more: your connection with God. You will find that you have never lost your loving, eternal connection with God even after all the pain and anguish you may have endured.

Spiritual Awakening

Soul contracts often play a crucial role in triggering spiritual awakening, or remembering your true nature and purpose. These contracts can catalyze profound shifts in consciousness and lead you toward greater spiritual awareness.

Exploring Soul Contracts

It can be extremely healing and empowering to see your past relationships—romantic, familial, and otherwise—through the lens of soul contracts. To begin intuiting a deeper level within your impactful relationships and imagining yourself having chosen these relationships as a means to learn can allow you to see a deeper level of wisdom within the pain, joy, grief, love, and even victimization experienced in these bonds. Using this understanding to reflect upon your own life experience, relationships, and patterns with an open mind and intuition, you might begin to sense that there is another level at play within your relationships.

While the topic of soul contracts is extremely personal, many find solace, guidance, and empowerment through learning more about this belief. It allows you to take accountability for what you need to learn and see, especially when it comes to what you think.

When you hurt someone else, you often carry guilt and shame around it even after you have changed your behavior. The same goes for when you have been victimized by someone and are unable to leave the event in the past. In both cases, thinking of the experience as something that has been decided in a soul contract allows you to feel your feelings, grieve the experience, and move forward into the present. It allows you to take accountability for your actions and extract the lessons you need from the experience.

Soul contracts offer a framework for understanding why certain people enter your life and why certain experiences unfold the way they do. They remind you that nothing is random, that your soul chose this journey with intention, and that every encounter—painful or joyful—serves your evolution. By embracing this perspective, you can transform your relationships from sources of confusion or suffering into profound teachers, guiding you back to your divine nature and your connection with God.

As we'll explore in the next chapter, while your soul navigates these contracts and lessons, it does so through a physical vessel that requires care and attention. Understanding the mind-body relationship means honoring the body that carries your consciousness through this lifetime.

Chapter Seven

The Mind-Body Relationship

> *"The best 9 doctors: sunshine, water, rest, air, sleep, exercise, meditation, diet, and good company."*
>
> — @believe.in.buddha

Your body is a gift from God.

You are born into a unique body that carries you through life. Depending on how you treat it, this body can either serve you or imprison you. It is helpful to view it as a temple, the place from which all your experiences, sensations, stories, and dreams emerge. How you treat this temple and how you allow others to treat it is ultimately your choice.

If you were to take a snapshot of your body at this

moment, you could say that your body, both internally and externally, reflects a historical account of your consciousness and habits up to this point. It records the history of your choices.

If your body doesn't feel like a comfortable place to inhabit right now, you can take action to shift your perception. By doing so, you can transform both your internal experience and your external appearance. Internal well-being naturally manifests outwardly, and conversely, by pursuing external fitness, you cultivate internal wellness.

To feel fit internally, you must be at peace with yourself, your choices, and your habits. This encompasses how you care for your temple, what you nourish it with, the thoughts you entertain, and even the music you listen to. The saying "you are what you eat" extends to everything you expose yourself to.

Several factors can be used to measure your physical wellness, including heart rate, blood pressure, and energy levels. These factors are influenced by various aspects of your lifestyle, such as how well you sleep, the quality of the food you consume, the frequency of your exercise, the relationships you engage in, and even your history of trauma and the resources you have for healing.

Let's start with sleep.

Sleep and Restoration

Sleep is a key ingredient for a happy, healthy body. If you aren't getting sufficient, sound sleep each night, the quality of your days and body begins to reflect this. Your internal physiology and the external appearance of your body are directly related to how much you sleep.

Around 2001, due to highly stressful circumstances, the quality of my sleep started to deteriorate, and I began to experience insomnia. I visited my doctor, who prescribed a heavy sleep medication to help induce deeper rest, which I continued to use for the next fifteen years. For some reason, around December 2016, I noticed a drastic change taking place in my mind. The sleep medication I had been taking was altering my brain chemistry, and as a result, I began to experience intense anxiety, fear, and depression like I had never faced before. I believe it was all due to my prolonged use of this medication. The fear became so maddening that I didn't want to be in my home of thirteen years alone at night.

My best friend Jenny became concerned for me, and she knew we needed to do something immediately to help me get off this heavy sleep medication and reclaim my peace and sleep.

Jenny is a talented herbalist, and thanks to her knowledge, she and I were successful in creating an all-natural sleep supplement that gradually repaired the neurons in my brain, promoting better sleep. My neurological chemistry took about 150 days to heal and allow for healthy sleep again, and during this time, I could not sleep more than an hour or two each night while the neurons in my brain had a chance to repair. This was one of the most challenging experiences I've ever faced.

Jenny was a godsend. She stayed by my side throughout the entire ordeal, counseling and supporting me through each difficult moment. During this process, we developed an all-natural sleep product called My Healthy Sleep, which consists of five amino acids and five herbs with no artificial ingredients.

Food and Nutrition

What you put into your body affects how you feel, how you think, and how you show up each day.

And yet, in today's world, much of what we call "food" is actually working against us.

The Obesity Epidemic

Across the world, societies are facing an alarming rise in obesity and lifestyle-related illnesses. What was once considered unusual has become the norm. The United States is one of the clearest examples of this trend—a country where food has become more about convenience and profit than nourishment.

The epidemic of obesity in the US is a systemic, political, and capitalistic issue in every respect. While the systemic roots of obesity are outside the scope of this book, I encourage you to do your own personal research into the deregulation of our food safety and health systems by processed and fast food companies; the gutting of regulatory systems by money in politics; and the distancing of communities from their local sources of nutrition. Organic, healthy food is difficult to access in the US. Where healthy food is available, it is not as cheap or as widely marketed as less nutritious food options.

The result of these toxic systems is people choosing unhealthy food sources and often eating to excess without understanding the impact of what it's doing to their bodies. Not only does it show up in weight-related health issues, but it also makes it unlikely that one can participate easily in one's own day-to-day life. There are more people with limited mobility, in wheelchairs, using canes, and experiencing difficulty breathing than we've ever seen before, imprisoned in unhealthy bodies. In 1990, about 11.6 percent of adults in the US were obese, according to the CDC and American Health Rankings.[1] In 2021, that

1. America's Health Rankings, "Obesity Through the Years,"

number soared to around 40 percent.[2] Imagine where this number will be in ten years.

Not surprisingly, child obesity is another epidemic in the US, with a prevalence of about 20 percent in April 2024.[3] When children are raised in environments where obesity is the norm of family, extended family, and community, their consciousness holds the belief that this is the norm of society, and their habits will follow this belief. When parents decide to focus on their own health and well-being, their shift in consciousness creates a new belief and example for their children, demonstrating that health and fitness are achievable and accessible. In turn, this creates a new belief and example for their children's consciousness that health and fitness are achievable and accessible.

The incidence of obesity is alarming. At this rate, it is quite obvious that there is a systems issue, and despite the odds, a healthy consciousness and awareness can help us keep our bodies fit and healthy individually, communally,

---

September 9, 2019, https://www.americashealthrankings.org/learn/news/obesity-through-the-years.

2. S. D. Emmerich, C. D. Fryar, B Stierman, and C. L. Ogden, "Obesity and Severe Obesity Prevalence in Adults: United States, August 2021–August 2023," CDC Stacks, NCHS Data Brief, no. 508 (September 24, 2024), https://dx.doi.org/10.15620/cdc/159281.

3. CDC, "Childhood Obesity Facts," Centers for Disease Control and Prevention, April 2, 2024, https://www.cdc.gov/obesity/childhood-obesity-facts/childhood-obesity-facts.html.

and systemically. It starts with you and me choosing what we feed ourselves every day.

Once this is acknowledged, through consciousness you can become more intentional about food choices—selecting options that nourish rather than harm—within whatever means and resources are available.

Luckily, if we are currently making unhealthy food choices, we can choose healthier ones by developing awareness about what we are putting in our bodies and how food makes us feel.

Take a minute to ponder this question: Do you eat to live, or do you live to eat? A vast amount of the human race lives to eat, and that's creating an unhealthy and dangerous epidemic here on Earth.

Food is our energy source, which means we're not meant to live for it—but to live because of it.

Poor Choices and Emotional Eating

Many years ago, I worked with a man who became a good friend, who I'll call Joseph. Joseph weighed 380 pounds, and we worked together on a plan to help him lose weight. Over six months, he lost thirty pounds. Unfortunately, he couldn't maintain the new lifestyle choices needed to keep his new body. Joseph gained back all the weight and then some.

If you've ever started a new "diet" without shifting the

deeper belief about yourself, you've probably seen how quickly old habits return. When your consciousness hasn't changed, your results can't last. The secret lies in what you believe about yourself. The relationship between your consciousness and your body is one of the most powerful tools you have in creating lasting health.

One day, Joseph and I went to lunch at a healthy salad bar. I watched him fill his plate with fresh vegetables, protein, and whole grains. As we reached the end of the buffet line, he picked up a glass and began to fill it with Coca-Cola.

I asked him what he was thinking at that moment, after all the progress he'd made. He said, "I had a hard day; I deserve it."

That was a WOW moment. Joseph's mind was revealing how stress and discomfort can trigger an old belief—that something sweet will make you feel better. In that moment, he wasn't feeding his body; he was trying to soothe emotional pain.

Many of us do the same thing. We eat to ease emotions we haven't yet faced. We reach for comfort, not nourishment. But when you decide to change those patterns, you're choosing to face discomfort head-on, with only the new consciousness you have been choosing to develop.

If you can give evidence to the belief "I am healthy, I am fit, I am happy," you create a new pathway in your consciousness. That pathway must be strengthened over time through consistent mental fitness and repetition. When stress arises and the old patterns resurface, you'll need to choose again and again until your new belief becomes stronger than the old one.

Even after losing thirty pounds, Joseph couldn't sustain his progress because the belief underneath hadn't changed. To him, being kind to himself still meant soothing stress with sugar instead of supporting his health.

Real self-kindness is choosing what truly supports your well-being—even when it's hard.

Living in the Moment

Another friend of mine provides a further example of consciousness and health-related habits. "David" was an excellent Certified Public Accountant (CPA), a real happy-go-lucky guy. But he also loved smoking and drinking. He was always the "life of the party" and rarely held back. For David, life was all about "living in the moment."

I saw firsthand the toll that "living in the moment" took on him. Living in the moment is vital, but it's not about indulging in what destroys the body. It's about living fully—feeling both the joy and the discomfort that exist in the present—without turning away. When you allow both pleasure and pain, you open the door to a deeper, steadier joy. True energy and vitality come from not avoiding what's real.

David was still young when he passed away. He never paid attention to the simple choices that could have supported his health—cutting back on drinking and smoking, or stopping altogether. Being the life of the party gave him joy, but it also consumed him.

David's example taught me the value of living in the moment in a healthy way—to give ourselves the best chance at a long, vibrant life.

When he passed away, his wife was heartbroken. She realized that his early death might have been prevented if he had developed a consciousness rooted in health and longevity. At the time, he was enjoying life, but he was living in a present without a future.

True presence means embracing all of what's here—the good and the difficult—and letting those experiences deepen your awareness. That's how you build a better future, moment by moment.

Whatever you desire is achievable, whether it's beneficial or detrimental to you. Every desire begins with the beliefs, thoughts, and images you hold about yourself. Your consciousness reflects these beliefs into reality without judgment and concern for whether your choices have a positive or destructive impact on your life.

Exercise and Movement

My Own Body Struggle

In my early thirties, during a ski trip, I had a rude awakening about my physical fitness. I hadn't realized how out of shape I'd become until, after one run, I conked out for over an hour. Since that day, I've been on an imperfect but intentional journey to treat my body and mind with more care. It hasn't been a straight path by any means.

About five years ago, I found myself roughly twenty pounds heavier than I wanted to be. I worked out regularly, rode my bike every day, and considered myself healthy—but when I looked in the mirror, there it was: the belly. I'd admire my arms and chest and think, "Looking good!" Then I'd see my stomach and groan. That single detail managed to overshadow all my progress.

Having worked in fitness for years, I knew what was possible, and I also knew the first obstacle wasn't physical, it was in my consciousness. Once I got honest about that, I set a clear intention to lose twenty pounds. Within two months, I did it.

It wasn't just about looking better, it was about feeling better. I want to feel strong, vibrant, and yes, sexy, at any age. And while I love sweets and fresh bread as much as anyone, I value a healthy, energized body even more. I think not only about how long I want to live, but how I want to live. I never want to feel trapped inside a body I've neglected. I give to my body so it can give back to me for many years to come.

Being the perfectionist (and sometimes impatient human) that I am, I chose a fast route: intermittent fasting and calorie reduction. I ate my first meal at noon and had my last meal at around 6 p.m. That rhythm worked for me. You might choose a slower route, and that's okay! What matters most is the shift in consciousness: aligning your mindset with your desire for health. Five years later, I'm still in shape, and honestly, I feel sexy again at the young age of sixty-eight.

These days, I don't just want to look good for now. I want to create the best version of myself before I die because that's where I'll begin my next lifetime.

Getting Started with Exercise

You don't need a fancy gym or a personal trainer to start moving your body (though it's great if you have access to those resources)! What matters most is consistency: finding something that gets your blood flowing and feels sustainable for you. Whether it's walking, stretching, dancing in your living room, or lifting weights at the gym, the goal is simply to move with intention.

Personally, I'd rather deal with the short-term discomfort of sore muscles and the withdrawal from sugar and processed foods than face the long-term consequences of illness, doctors, and hospital visits. I'm grateful that medical care exists, but I'd rather not need it if I can help it.

To keep myself motivated, I often visualize what it would feel like to live in a body weighed down by poor choices. That image pushes me to make better ones. Every day, I remind myself that how I care for my body today determines how much I'll get to live tomorrow.

If your goal is to exercise more, start small. A ten-minute walk each day is enough to build momentum. You might feel sore or out of shape at first, but stick with it. Soon, you'll notice that movement feels good again, and your body will thank you.

The "Ideal" Body Type

To change the way our bodies look, we must change the way we look at our bodies.

Capitalistic marketing schemes have portrayed a uniform, often impossible and unhealthy, image of the "ideal" body type. On billboards and advertisements, we are presented with a specific body type with ripped 6-pack abs or with 4 percent body fat, leading people into all forms of body dysmorphia. First, there are as many body types as human beings, and it is literally impossible for two humans to look the same, even using identical health regimens. Moreover, our bodies reflect our activities. They will look one way if we play basketball and a remarkedly different way if we run long-distance marathons. The only goal of physical fitness that I believe is worth setting is to create a body for yourself that feels healthy and happy from the inside while engaging in the activities and lifestyle you enjoy most.

By becoming creative with our own diet and exercise habits, we can create a body that we feel light and joyful inside of. To do this, we can visualize how we want to look, how we want to feel, and even how much energy we want to have throughout the day—creating the body we desire from the present. This process will begin to attract our attention to foods and activities most aligned with this feeling and visualization.

When a person creates a body they feel happy and healthy inside of, there is a light vibrancy to them. They feel differently than someone in pain and imprisoned in an unhealthy body. This is an extremely personal process. There are many factors that are out of our control when it comes to the size and health of our bodies, yet, much is in our control.

No matter the shape and size of your body today, you

can feel good inside of it by feeding it healthy food and moving/exercising it in accordance with your own limits. You can utilize your consciousness to aid your journey toward a healthier and fitter body. By beginning to think, feel, and visualize yourself internally as healthy, feeling good, and looking good, your external activities and habits will begin to reflect this.

Relationships and Support

The relationships you engage in have a profound impact on your body and mind. My friend Jenny's presence during my sleep medication crisis exemplifies how crucial supportive relationships are to happiness and health. Without her support, knowledge, and commitment, I might not have made it through that challenging time.

Our relationships can lift us higher or drain our energy. My friend James is a perfect example of someone who elevates everyone around him. He is ablaze with an aura of love and authenticity. When you're in his presence, it feels like standing in the sun. That kind of energy isn't accidental; it's the result of the inner work he's done on his own consciousness, health, and self-awareness.

When you take care of yourself, you naturally extend that care to others. Your own vitality becomes a light that supports the people around you. This is why it's crucial to surround yourself with people who encourage your growth. Find those who celebrate your progress, who remind you of your strength when you forget. A friend, family member, or workout partner who shares your values can keep you inspired and accountable.

Caring for your body and shifting your consciousness is one of the greatest gifts you can give yourself and those you love. When you feel good, your energy ripples outward. You show up more fully for your kids, grandkids, and friends. You have more to give. As soon as you work on shifting your consciousness, you naturally become a tool of light to help all those that come in contact with you!

Only you have the power to choose: Will you move through life exhausted and disconnected, barely making it through the day, or will you cultivate the energy to live, play, and love fully?

Healing from Past Patterns and Trauma

What's "Normal" to You?

What was your home environment like as a child?

How did your family handle emotions? Through conversation, silence, or avoidance?

What relationship with food was fostered in your home?

How did the adults around you approach rest, stress, or self-care?

Who were your role models growing up? Who taught you how to take care of yourself, how to love, how to rest?

The truth is, much of what we call "normal" comes from what we've seen repeated around us. We are, in many ways, products of our early environments and the people we've spent the most time with. Even when our bodies try to speak to us—through fatigue, discomfort, or joy—we can't always hear those signals beneath the noise of old conditioning.

Maybe you grew up in a home where processed foods, television, smoking, or drinking were everyday habits. Over time, that lifestyle becomes familiar, passed down from generation to generation until poor health feels ordinary. In contrast, families who value activity, whole foods, and mindful living create a consciousness where vitality feels natural and imbalance feels out of place.

As humans, we tend to cling to what feels familiar, even when it no longer serves us. Healing begins when you notice those inherited patterns and ask yourself, *Does this version of normal align with who I want to be now?*

My wish for you is to find your own definition of normal, a way of living that honors your present self. Keep what nurtures you from the past, and gently release what doesn't serve your health or happiness anymore.

Food as a Reward

One powerful way to understand how early conditioning shapes your adulthood is to examine your relationship with food. Think about the reward systems many families use—doctors giving lollipops after well-behaved visits or parents offering sweets when you're sad. These seemingly innocent moments create deep associations in your consciousness at a young age. Food becomes a reward, a punishment, or an emotional regulator.

What happens when an old habit becomes dysfunctional? So many of us experience cravings after meals for sweet desserts—ice cream, cake, cookies, or some kind of snack laden with sugar—even if intellectually in our minds we know that it is unhealthy to conclude all meals with sugary sweets. The association is so strongly ingrained from childhood that it takes a mighty will to simply finish a meal and not cap it off with a sugary dessert.

This pattern isn't about blame. Your parents and grandparents likely expressed genuine love through food. My own grandmother's first words when I visited were, "You know where the cookie jar is!" That was true love from her heart.

But recognizing where these associations began allows you to heal them. When you notice yourself reaching for food to manage emotions or seeking that post-meal reward, you're witnessing an old pattern, one formed in childhood that no longer needs to control your adult choices.

Resources for Healing

Do you want something different?

If you're reading this book right now, reflecting on the health of your body, spirit, and mind, and noticing the unhealthy aspects, embrace the present moment and the joy of awareness. Anything and everything can be changed through your understanding of consciousness, where your most fundamental beliefs live.

The hardest part will be developing the discipline to change your old narrative and what you subconsciously consider "normal." There presently exists a distance between your current reality and the reality you desire, and every time you take an action in alignment with what you desire, your "old normal" will rear its head, telling you to back down. Please don't! Your life can actually depend on it.

The Power of Habit Formation and Shifting Your Consciousness

> "*Every day, you have two choices: to focus on what's wrong or to embrace what's right. Choose gratitude, choose joy, choose to see the beauty in the little things and life will become even more incredible than you imagined.*
>
> — @soul.healing.guidance

Habit formation is the process by which we create new structures to guide our actions away from the "old normal" and into our "desired normal." Habits are mental and emotional frameworks that allow you to perform tasks on autopilot, conserving energy and freeing up mental space. Our habits are not us, and this is the key! You can survey them impersonally to see what needs changing.

Sometimes, as I sit and watch people go about their day—driving, walking, working—I can't help but wonder: *What brought them here? What choices or experiences shaped who they've become? Where are they headed?*

Consciousness is the totality of who we believe ourselves to be. When people struggle to take care of themselves, it's often because they feel stuck in human-consciousness, without access to God-consciousness, the deeper dimension of awareness and truth where genuine transformation begins.

Let's take smoking as an example. Many people who smoke don't just see it as something they do; they see it as part of who they are. They've built an identity around it —"I am a smoker." So when they try to quit, they're not just fighting a behavior; they're fighting a self-concept. Quitting feels impossible because, on a subconscious level, they're trying to stop being who they believe they are!

The shift begins when a person stops identifying as a smoker and starts identifying as a nonsmoker. This is what I mean by shifting your consciousness. It's not simply about breaking a habit; it's about changing the way you define yourself within your own awareness. And this applies to all areas of life—health, weight, relationships, abundance, and beyond.

Making that shift requires honesty and courage. You may have to face the emotions and memories that led to the habit in the first place. These are the hidden triggers that keep old behaviors alive. But when you face them with compassion, you take your power back. You begin to act from awareness rather than reaction.

Once you've made that inner shift, simple habits can anchor it into your everyday. For example, if your goal is to feel healthy, connect with your emotions when you're eating and notice how the food makes you feel in the minutes and hours afterward.

After you establish your goal, break it down into smaller, more manageable actions. This approach can make the goal feel less overwhelming and increase your chances of success. Write everything down, including the main goal and the smaller steps. Treat it like a creative project and have fun with it!

Another key aspect of habit formation is creating a supportive environment to reinforce your new habits. This includes removing barriers to regular physical movement, whether you choose to exercise at home, outside, or wherever works best for you.

To reinforce the habit, establish a reward system similar to the one used to create the habits you're trying to replace. Perhaps after completing a week of healthy eating and exercising consistently, you can treat yourself to something that reinforces your new direction—time in nature, a favorite healthy meal, or simply acknowledging how far you've come.

Finally, stay committed to the habit even when faced with setbacks or challenges. It's natural to experience setbacks when forming new habits, and it's crucial to recognize that they are an opportunity to learn and grow.

Living in God-consciousness takes determination and persistence, but it's from this place that you can create the life you've always dreamed of. Every time you choose presence over autopilot, truth over comfort, love over fear, you change! One thought, one breath, one choice at a time, you reshape your consciousness into the most beautiful version of yourself.

Short-Term Discomfort over Long-Term Pain

To change a habit, you will need to face short-term discomfort.

Looking back at the example I used earlier in this chapter about the family that eats too much processed food and sweets, imagine how uncomfortable it might be to stop eating these addictive types of foods cold turkey. They might feel deprived, as though everything good has been taken away.

Most people either don't start taking care of themselves because they feel it's too hard, or they don't know how to get started because it's totally different from anything they've tried in the past. They may get frustrated and quit during the short-term discomfort phase.

If these things start happening to you, learn to push through the uncomfortable moments until you have shifted your consciousness and arrived on the other side to a happier, healthier you.

For most of us who want to feel healthier in our bodies, it's because many habits, experiences, and beliefs throughout our lives have created patterns that don't serve our well-being. Within the scope of what's possible for your unique body and circumstances, you can decide to shift your consciousness to support the health and vitality available to you.

To improve your body's health, start with habits that support your well-being, one hour and day at a time, and slowly your consciousness will shift to reflect a version of you that feels more aligned with your desired well-being.

Being overweight is hard
Being physically fit is hard
Choose your hard.

Being in debt is hard.
Being financially disciplined is hard.
Choose your hard.

Working a 9 to 5 until you're 65 years old is hard.
Starting a business is hard.
Choose your hard

A careless life without God is hard.
A life dedicated to God is hard.
Choose your hard.

You see, life is never easy.
It's hard by nature,
and the only thing you have to do is choose your hard.

So choose wisely.

—@morrischestnutofficial

Understanding Consciousness and Health Through Aging

While hormones, age, and genetics play a crucial role in our bodies, what is always in your control is what you have been feeding your consciousness day in and day out since you were born.

Whatever is manifesting in your life at the moment—whether it's the way you're feeling or anything else—is a direct result of all that you're allowing into yourself, from your food to your habits to your thoughts.

Our bodies are here to serve and support us in a healthy, happy way, yet many people's bodies bring them great suffering. To deal with this suffering, you must become conscious of the root of your suffering, and from that position, utilize free will and free choice to create and manifest what you truly desire.

What Happens to Our Bodies as We Age?

> “*Everything is super important until you are sick. Then you realize there was only ever one thing that was important, your health.*
>
> — @buddhaquotes__

Life is created from our mindsets. By working to create healthy mindsets today, you're investing in an asset that pays dividends until the end of your life. By avoiding the admittedly difficult work and commitment to creating a mind and body that will serve you throughout your later days, you're more likely to become imprisoned within a body that naturally perpetuates the mindset you created early on—an unhealthy one.

To be "imprisoned" in an unhealthy body is to be unable to engage in your day-to-day activities in a way that feels good to you. Naturally, we will all eventually lose some ability to function—our eyesight will worsen with time and our bodies will weaken. This is natural and to be celebrated as well; it is a season of life. The work at hand is not about fighting this process but about being flexible enough in your thinking and habits to live every moment deeply and vibrantly. To do this, you need to understand that many diseases are merely symptoms of habits and not aging. By changing those habits through consciousness, you can avoid early bodily destruction and disability.

Looking around, I notice that the natural aging process has been accelerated and validated with beliefs such as "I must be getting old," "That's just what happens at X age," or beliefs that getting older means needing mobility aids or medical equipment. There has been a mass acceptance of early-onset disability and bodily decay.

Certain ages are equated with sickness and infirmity when it doesn't have to be this way.

It's possible to choose and shift your consciousness at any moment. No matter your current age or the condition of your body, you can change the environmental factors within your control to work with your body and create a life that feels vibrant to you, improving the process one day at a time. Whether you're managing chronic pain, physical limitations, or starting from a place of being out of shape, the goal isn't perfection. It's progress that honors where you are right now.

In my case, my mind tends to look into the future, focusing on the big picture and forecasting, based on my current behaviors, what the rest of my days will look and feel like. If I don't take care of myself day by day—mentally, physically, and spiritually—I won't have the future I want when I get older.

My mantra is to live in a loving, happy, healthy, wealthy, and wise way up to the ripe old age of 110 years old or MORE! After having set my mind to financial prosperity at a young age and achieving it at the age of fifty-seven, I now want to live long and healthy and enjoy my body for many years to come!

The Ways Our Body Represents Our Consciousness

Another example of an unhealthy belief is the way cancer and illness are viewed in our society. In *Dying to Be Me*,[4] Moorjani says that "cancer is just a word that creates fear [...] All illnesses are just symptoms of imbalance. No illness can remain when your entire system is in balance." While the scientific mechanisms of cancer are complex—involving genetic mutations, environmental factors, and processes not fully understood—many holistic health practitioners believe that our mindset and stress levels can influence our body's resilience.

Cancer cells do not always result in sickness or metastasis; it is only when they begin to attack a section of our body that they cause disease and danger. This suggests that we have much more control over our health than we often realize.

Moreover, when cancer is diagnosed, patients are frequently led to believe that it's simply a matter of having the disease and accepting it. Many do not consider how their lifestyle choices might have contributed to the development of cancer in the first place, nor do they recognize what aspects of their health are still within their control. By failing to take ownership of their body and their

4. Anita Moorjani, *Dying to Be Me*.

mindset regarding cancer or any other disease, individuals may inadvertently contribute to their own illnesses.

The habits that create our consciousness play a crucial role in addressing diseases, such as cancer, and working toward stabilization. For example, "emerging evidence suggests that fasting could play a key role in cancer treatment by fostering conditions that limit cancer cells' adaptability, survival, and growth."[5] Too many people leave their health completely in the hands of their doctor rather than taking a holistic approach, working alongside their doctor to create better habits, mindsets, and lifestyles to prevent cancer or other diseases, or in cases of actual diagnosis, help support healing.

If you take care of your body and do everything possible to prevent disease, you may avoid living imprisoned in an unhealthy body and enjoy a vibrant one.

---

5. Sagun Tiwari, Sapkota Namrata, and Han Zhenxiang, "Effect of Fasting on Cancer: A Narrative Review of Scientific Evidence," *Cancer Science* 113, no. 10 (August 2022): 3291–3302, https://pmc.ncbi.nlm.nih.gov/articles/PMC9530862/.

Final Reflections

> *"You have been talking to the universe all your life without even realizing it, and it has been listening to you."*
>
> — @spirituallyalign

I believe you can live in a truly magical and abundant way. Let this book serve as your inspiration to create a life for yourself that truly reflects your inner desires.

I hope that through sharing my own spiritual journey, I have provided the spark for you to take the leap of faith and start shifting your consciousness today.

My mantra is to live my life in a *Loving, Happy, Healthy, Wealthy, and Wise way.*

Loving means sharing love in all my connections, present and future.

Happy means smiling and accessing joy daily.

Healthy means living in a vibrant body.

Wealthy means having enough money to care for myself for the rest of my life and enough wealth to share with many, many others along the way.

Wise means maintaining a sharp, engaged mind—one that continues to grow intellectually.

I'm sure I will reach my goals because I'm training my consciousness every day to be the best version of myself I can possibly be!

I believe that you too can do that.

I believe in you, and love you, for you are me, and we are one.

May your journey in this lifetime be filled with Love, Happiness, Health, Wealth, and Wisdom!

May you prosper in every imaginable way.

> *"In India when we meet and part we often say, 'Namasté,' which means: I honor the place in you where the entire universe resides; I honor the place in you of love, of light, of truth, of peace. I honor the place within you where, if you are in that place in you, and I am in that place in me, there is only one of us. Namasté."*
>
> — Ram Dass

What does angel number 1111 mean?

1111 is a message from the angelic energies
that you are supported by forces you cannot see.
It gives you confirmation that everything is on schedule
and divinely guided in your world.

Afterword

What was the true purpose behind religion being created?

Religion wasn't created to connect you to God. It was created to control your connection to God. In ancient times, spiritual knowledge was something every human had access to. People lived in rhythm with nature, they could feel the presence of the divine within their breath, their body, their heart. But as civilizations grew, leaders realized something powerful: if you can control what people believe, you can control how they behave. So they built systems that took mystical teachings like the words of Christ, Buddha, Krishna, and they institutionalized them. They turned living wisdom into doctrine. They told people, "God is out there, you're separate. You're a sinner. You need us, the church, the priest, the temple to reach Him." And that's how humanity slowly lost its direct connection to the divine. The masses were easier to manipulate when they felt guilty, small, and afraid of eternal punishment. Fear became the ultimate form of control.

But here's the truth: no religion owns God. God is not in a book, a building, or a ritual. God is within you: the breath in your lungs, the love in your chest, the stillness in your mind... that's the living presence of Source.

The true awakening happening on Earth right now is humanity remembering. You don't need permission to connect to the divine. You are the divine remembering itself. We all truly are the divine remembering itself and more and more of us are awakening to that. And now is our time to truly awaken to the fact that God is not outside of us, not something that we have to worship to. It is within us, and the more that we connect to our divine self, the more that we recognize that together.

– @jake_whan

Religious people's worst fear is not hell. It is not sin. It's the idea that everything that they have been taught might not be true. Because if they were to actually question it, if they were truly to look behind the walls of religion, their entire reality would shatter. They'd have to face the terrifying truth that God is not outside of them, that the people that they gave their power to were never divine intermediaries. That heaven and hell were never places, they were states of consciousness, and that's what most people can't handle. The death of the false self. It's easier to follow rules than to face your own divinity. It is easier to obey than to awaken.

You see, religion has always played one clever game: convince them they are sinners then have them pay to be forgiven. And once you believe that you are unworthy of God, you become dependent on the very system that took your power away in the first place. That is how control is maintained - not through violence, but through belief.

But when you start remembering who you truly are, you feel the divine inside your own being. You can't be controlled anymore. You no longer live from fear—you live from truth. And that is what terrifies the system, because an awakened soul cannot be manipulated. So religious people's worst fear is that one day they're going to wake up and recognize that they were never separate from God at all.

– @jake_whan

Acknowledgments

I've had many uniquely incredible and varying beacons of light guiding me toward my goal—having the success and prosperity that God intended me to obtain and realize from the very beginning.

In writing this book, I believe God is using me as a conduit to help others adjust and shift their consciousness so that they can receive ALL the abundant glory the Universe has to offer.

Perhaps this book might serve as a beacon for you as well.

Throughout my life, I've continually sought out inspiring people. I would like to express my immense gratitude to my best friend, Jenny Felice. I would also like to thank Anita Moorjani, Joel Goldsmith, Reverend Al Heard, Reverend Jim Lewis, Dr. Roger Teel, and Sadhguru—a few of the many souls who have inspired and uplifted me along my earthbound journey.

But most of all, I would like to give thanks to God for the incredible journey He has created for me in this incarnation.

www.ingramcontent.com/pod-product-compliance
Lightning Source LLC
LaVergne TN
LVHW090609110826
845146LV00001B/317

* 9 7 9 8 2 1 8 8 8 2 0 7 5 *